can't sell
won't sell

Also by the author:

How to do better creative work;
First published by Pearson Education Limited in 2009

Changing the world is the only fit work for a grown man;
First published by Adworld Press in 2012

How to write better copy;
First published by Macmillan/Bluebird Books in 2016

Um conto de duas cidades (A tale of two cities);
First published by Blue Book in 2019

can't sell won't sell

Advertising, politics and culture wars
Why adland has stopped selling
and started saving the world

ADWORLD
PRESS

First published in the United Kingdom in April, 2020 by Adworld Press. Second edition published in August, 2020.

Third edition published August, 2021.

ISBN 978-0-9571515-2-9

Steve Harrison

Steve was European Creative Director (OgilvyOne) and Global Creative Director (Wunderman) either side of starting his own agency, HTW, where, in the seven years the agency operated, he won more Cannes Lions (18) in his discipline than any creative director in the world. His work has subsequently featured in *The D&AD Copy Book*. He has also authored *Changing the world is the only fit work for a grown man; How to write better copy;* and *How to do better creative work* – the latter becoming the most expensive advertising book ever when it traded on Amazon for £3,854 a copy.

For Tommy, Olive and Mo

Foreword

When I started as a copywriter, the benefit of advertising was explained to me in a sentence: "It's what you do when you can't afford to send a salesman."

For clients with a large inventory that needed shifting, a new product that needed launching, a workforce that needed to be kept in gainful employment and a wage bill that needed to be met, it was a convincing reason to hire an agency.

Today there are many in our industry who prefer this: "Advertising is what you do when you can't afford to send someone from Diversity, Inclusion and Sustainability."

Which, if you have a large inventory that needs shifting, a new product that needs launching, a workforce that needs to be kept in gainful employment and a wage bill that needs to be met, isn't quite as appealing.

And it's even less so when your business has been hit by a catastrophic pandemic, and you are trying to work your way out of the ensuing recession.

Some comments on the
first edition of *Can't Sell Won't Sell*

"A clear indictment of something that's gone badly wrong with the ad business, and an urgent call to put it right." *Paul Feldwick, Author, "The Anatomy of Humbug" and "Why Does the Pedlar Sing?"*

"A highly provocative plea for less uniformity and greater diversity of thought in advertising." *Orlando Wood, Author, "Lemon. How the Advertising Brain Turned Sour".*

"Little has caused me to think about our industry and where we are at more recently than *Can't Sell, Won't Sell.* This is a fascinating and incredibly researched piece of work." *Richard Huntington, Chairman and Chief Strategy Officer, Saatchi & Saatchi London Group.*

"It constantly made me go 'Yes, yes. I think that but I didn't realise I thought it until you just said it'." *Paul Burke, Writer, Producer and Director.*

"This is a welcome – and timely – reminder that our industry has lost the plot. Steve calls 'bullshit' on those lazy, right-on individuals and companies who have lost touch with commercial reality." *Jon Steel, Author, "Truth, Lies & Advertising", and "Perfect Pitch".*

"Steve expertly dissects the major problems at the heart of an underperforming industry that is bound up in its own self-worth, and fails to understand the very people it seeks to engage and influence." *Andrew Tenzer, Director of Market Insight & Brand Strategy at Reach Plc.*

"Even if you disagree with all of it, you'd be crazy to miss out on analysing his argument." *Marc Lewis, Dean, School of Communication Arts.*

"An excellent book which encapsulates the problem powerfully and backs it up with sources and numbers. It would be good for our industry if lots of agencies buy it and distribute it to their staff." *Dave Trott, Creative Director, Copywriter, Author.*

"If advertising is going to stop sleepwalking into obsolescence, this is the wake-up call it needs." *Dave Dye, Chief Creative Officer, LOVE or FEAR and author, "Stuff From the Loft".*

Acknowledgements

If this book is likely to lose me a few industry friends, then I'm fortunate that others have rallied round while I've been writing it.

First up, Patrick Collister. As you'll see from the opening paragraph, he got me started. Actually, it all began nearly two years ago when he asked me to make the speech at his Caples Awards ceremony. It was there that I introduced the argument you're about to read. I thought he (along with most of the audience) would be offended, but far from it. Patrick said I should develop the idea and has since encouraged me to do so, and fed me some startling stats from his *Cannes Conflicted* report. He really is the most generous man in advertising.

I've also been fortunate to get help and advice from Tom Callaghan. Tom is the best copywriter I know. He now makes a living crafting best-selling detective fiction but, for the past few months, has been correcting my many crimes against the English language.

For forensic research, I'm indebted to my old mate, the neuropsychologist, Marcus McGinty. Amongst many other revelations, he turned me on to Jonathan Haidt, and has sent me essential despatches from the front line of the culture wars throughout this entire process. Long may our correspondence continue.

I've had tough but helpful criticism from Martin Bihl over in the US, and got mind-expanding insight from Orlando Wood (incidentally, what he and the IPA did with *Lemon* was adland's most significant initiative of 2019). I've also benefited from Andrew Tenzer and Ian Murray's research and analysis. Indeed, I've nothing but admiration for the way they've defiantly roasted a complacent and out-of-touch industry. Of course, the doyen of that school is Mark Ritson, and his columns in *Marketing Week* have provided the theoretical backbone of this book.

Then there are my former colleagues David Macmillan, the Managing Director at Havas helia and Polly Jones, Global Client Partner at Wunderman/JWT. I asked them to fact-check chapter 8 so I didn't appear too up myself.

The task of reading the whole bloody thing, over and over and over again has fallen to my partner, Morag Brennan. Writing this book is just one of a thousand things I could not do without her. I've said it before and I'll say it again, I'm a very lucky man.

Once Mo had approved the 87th draft, it went to my publisher Miles Bailey and his colleagues, Rachel Woodman and Adrian Sysum. This is my fifth book, two of which have been published by them. They are the best.

And finally, while this book isn't meant to be funny, I'd like to mention two comic writers who've had a roundabout influence. The first is Italian writer, actor and comedian, Dario Fo. If you're familiar with his work, you'll recognise how I've re-purposed ... appropriated ... nicked the title of his play *Can't Pay? Won't Pay!* You'll also know that this farce is worth catching when next revived because it'll give you the only opportunity you'll ever get to use "Marxist" and "funny" in the same sentence.

The other comic inspiration has come from Ricky Gervais. Here's the closing of his 2020 Golden Globe speech, tweaked for the benefit of any potential Cannes Lions or D&AD winners: "If you do win an award tonight, don't use it as a platform to make a political speech. You're in no position to lecture the public about anything. You know nothing about the real world. So if you win, come up, accept your award, thank your client and your God, and fuck off, alright?"

Contents

1
Can't Sell
Won't Sell

The idea for this book came from a rather staggering statistic. It was given to me by my mate Patrick Collister, who edits and publishes *Directory* magazine.

Patrick was compiling his *Cannes Conflicted* analysis of the winners at 2019's advertising festival. And he discovered that, of the 28 entries that picked up a Grand Prix, only six of them had an increase in sales as an objective.[1]

It got us wondering if the people in our industry have lost the knack of selling – and, given the work they hold up as exemplary, if they actually care?

The same thoughts have no doubt occurred to their clients.

Back in April and June 2017, P&G trimmed between $100 – $140 million from its digital marketing costs, and nothing happened.

As Jon Moeller, the CFO explained: "We didn't see a reduction in growth rate (in value or volume of sales). What that tells me is that the spending we cut was largely ineffective."[2]

Huge as that $140 million budget might seem to you and me, it is simply the ad industry's problem in microcosm.

Fast forward to June 2019, and global consulting firm, Alix Partners, published their survey of 1,110 executives who work in consumer products companies in China,

France, Germany, India, the UK and the US. Their role is described as "digital transformation".

It appears they're not very good at it.

Of the $60 billion spent on digital advertising in 2018, around $30 billion had either a negative return or its return was not even measured. Overall, the report concluded that "approximately $50 billion of digital marketing and trade spend is wasted".[3]

If the analysts at Alix had been keeping up with another industry friend of mine, Bob Hoffmann, that insight wouldn't have come as too big a surprise.

The "digital delusion"

For over a decade, Bob has been writing about "the digital delusion" in his blog, *The Ad Contrarian*. His satirical barbs have skewered the digerati who promised us that their messages would be so targeted and so interactive that our prospects would eagerly embark on a long lasting and profitable virtual relationship.

Seth Godin is probably as responsible as anyone for foisting this fallacy upon us.

Way back in 1999 his *Permission Marketing* told us: "Interactive technology means that marketers can inexpensively engage consumers in one-to-one relationships fuelled by two-way 'conversations' ... Marketing in an interactive world is a collaborative activity—with the marketer helping the consumer to buy and the consumer helping the marketer to sell."[4]

"Bliss was it in that dawn to be alive," as Wordsworth

wrote of another revolution that promised much but failed greatly.

Unfortunately, as Bob Hoffman tells us, "you are more likely to complete Navy SEAL training than interact with a digital advertisement."[5]

That's because the main thing being sold by social media is false hope to gullible clients. According to Bob, the average click rate for banner ads is eight in 10,000, consumer engagement with Facebook posts is seven in 10,000, and with Twitter posts it's just three in 10,000.[6]

What makes these numbers so alarming is they reflect the [lack of] response of those who have actually opted in to receive these messages. These are not cold prospects. These are qualified leads.

Out with the old

Those who once scoffed at Bob are now eating their words. Alas, as he pointed out, the damage has been done and its effect on the industry has been systemic.

When digital hysteria was at its most frenzied, we were told we no longer needed a big idea that grabbed a prospect's attention and dramatised the benefit of the brand we were building or the product or service we were promoting.

Indeed, there'd be no need for a brief either, or the proposition that might be the focal point of that abruptive big idea.

As such, the ability to write either an advertising

strategy or a proposition disappeared from the skill set once found in most marketing organisations. As did any acknowledgement of their importance.

By 2016, the Fournaise Group, a world leader in measuring and tracking marketing effectiveness, found only 17% of marketers really got what a customer value proposition actually was.[7]

That's despite a clear proposition being the most crucial element in delivering "better effectiveness and better business results." [FYI: "It highlights the relevance of a product by explaining how it solves problems or improves the customer's situation."][8]

The other 83% of marketers interviewed by the Fournaise Group chose to ignore one of my favourite mantras: "If the brief isn't right the work won't be either". They preferred to focus on the creative.[9] Usually, however, on the proviso that that creative was turned round by end-of-play that day.

In fact, even those rush jobs would soon be cancelled. Because with the advent of SEO, there was no need for any creative at all. Google's software would do all the hard work for us.

"A crisis in creative effectiveness"

When clients started to question whether all this was quite the miracle the zealots said it would be, a new tech-driven belief system emerged: Big Data.

But this, too, has failed to lead us to the promised land. Indeed, the Institute of Practitioners in Advertising (IPA) now laments that this "golden age for advertising technology has been far from a golden age for advertising creativity".[10]

The IPA, which for years has been the industry's champion of work that works, recently ran an entire week of workshops and discussion groups on how to reverse "the crisis in creative effectiveness."

To focus minds, the IPA warned that "creatively awarded campaigns are now less effective than they have been in the entire 24-year run of data and are now no more effective than non-award-winning campaigns."[11]

Where once a creatively awarded campaign would be around 12 times as efficient as non-awarded ones, the multiplier was now in "catastrophic decline".[12]

As a further stimulus to the debate, the IPA published *Lemon, How the Advertising Brain Turned Sour* by System1's Chief Innovation Officer, Orlando Wood.[13] In this, the best advertising book in years, Wood offers his own explanation for why standards have nosedived. And it's all down to which side of the brain is governing our thinking and output.

According to him, individuals, agencies, businesses, and entire societies are susceptible to shifts between right and left brain thinking.

During periods when the former dominate, creativity flourishes. The right brain tells stories with an engaging mix of nuance and metaphor, word play and humour. And it leavens it with an all-important handful of empathy.

The left brain, however, is more literal, didactic and self-conscious, with a penchant for voice-overs telling the audience what to think.

Unfortunately, as Wood explains, that VO has been banging on with increasing intensity for most of this century. We'll return to what it says about the advertising we're currently producing on page 80. Meanwhile, Wood sees the work as "flat, abstract, dislocated and devitalised."[14]

And the industry in general? "What was once dazzling art form is now dreary science."[15]

"Stop living in la-la land"

Marketing Week's editor, Russell Parsons has reached the same conclusion about science's damaging effect. In June 2019 he told a gathering of seasoned b2b marketers: "Many have fled to a data-driven, digital dead end, afraid to take risks unless the master spreadsheet says it's OK".

As Russell explained, instead of effectiveness i.e. building brands and selling things, we've moved to efficiency. As a defensive measure in face of C-Level scepticism, CMOs have set about proving that the communications are giving more for less, and measuring that "more" in terms of "eyeballs, clicks, impressions, likes and shares".[16]

But as Jerome Fournaise, founder of the Fournaise Marketing Group warned long ago, such efficiency is not effectiveness. In setting these kind of targets, marketers are "mistaking engagement for conversion".

As he said back in 2014, they need to "stop living in la-la land and start behaving like real business people."[17] By that he meant actually setting out to segment and target their prospects, raise awareness, drive preference, and generate growth by selling to new customers and keeping old ones buying more.

My spirits rose when I came across an article in *The Drum* magazine titled "Goodbye to Likes: What Should the New Engagement Metric Be?" Alas there was no sign of "buy", "purchase", "sell" or "convert to sale" in any of the 929 words of advice.[18]

This kind of thinking is typical of those who live in la-la land. The problem is that, after fifteen years of digital dominance, the skills required to get people to "buy" or "purchase" our clients' goods and services barely exist on the agency side.

"Talking crap about Instagram and millennials"

You'd think clients would be alarmed by this. But the truth is, many Chief Marketing Officers have become as distracted and detached from the sales process as their agency counterparts.

This has not escaped the attention of their more business-like peers.

Forgive me wheeling out the admirably sales-oriented Fournaise Marketing Group one last time, but here they are on how bad it is in the boardroom: "We tracked that 80% of today's CEOs admit that they do not really trust and are not very impressed by the work done by their Marketers—while by comparison, 95% of those same CEOs do trust and value the opinion and work of CFOs and CIOs."[19]

No wonder really, is it?

As teacher, consultant and star columnist at *Marketing Week* Dr Mark Ritson says: "Talking crap about Instagram and millennials might get you to the top of the marketing ladder, but once you get to the big room on the top floor these superficial, tactical robes are quickly ripped away to reveal the naked imposter beneath.

"The CEO, CFO, CTO, CHRO, and general counsel look on with the bemused, embarrassed countenance of friends who have discovered you are still breast-feeding your 12-year-old."[20]

Regular columnist for *The Drum*, Samuel Scott agrees: "C-suite executives have every right not to take marketing seriously anymore. Why? Because our industry's alleged 'thought leaders' and top agencies say moronic things.

"Here are just a few that I have seen: 'The future of marketing is love.' 'We are where a more modern HOW happens.' 'The future of marketing is community.' 'It is about harnessing storyliving not storytelling.' 'We are a brand intimacy agency.' 'The key to content marketing is love'."[21]

These new age nostrums might seem deep and meaningful to marketeers. But CFOs and CEOs aren't feeling the love. And many have started dumping their CMOs.

At the time of writing, the role has already gone at Coca-Cola, Johnson & Johnson, McDonald's, Uber, Mondelez, Hyatt, Vodafone and in many other companies where it is being replaced by a Chief Growth Officer or someone of a much more commercial bent.

We all know new marketing brooms tend to sweep clean. But this time round, the new person in charge isn't putting the account up for pitch. They are taking it in-house.

Do it yourself

At P&G, the Chief Brand Officer, Marc Pritchard, declared: "It's time to disrupt the archaic 'Mad Men' model, eliminating silos between creatives, clients and consumers, and stripping away anything that doesn't add to the creative output ... We're now seizing back control".[22]

Tellingly, his efforts to "add to the creative output" have resulted in an 80% reduction in the number of agencies who'd been on his roster in 2015.[23]

Pritchard has particularly targeted those agencies who'd been planning and buying P&G's media. But, simultaneously hundreds of its creative ad, direct and digital agencies have also been culled.

Where P&G go others follow, and across every industry sector, clients have taken up DIY.

A simple explanation for this disregard for their agencies' talents was posited by Libby Brockhoff – one of the original founders of Mother and now the CEO of Odysseus Arms in San Francisco: "I believe that some of this change came from an underlying devaluation of what agencies do and a feeling that anyone with an ounce of creativity and Adobe Creative Suite could do it just as well."[24]

Marc Nohr, who is Chair of the IPA's Commercial Leadership Group, has suggested another reason for our clients' disillusion.

In his view, we see creative as an end in itself, and not as a means of achieving the client's fundamental business objective – which is to persuade people to buy their brand. As Marc says:

"Ask C-suite execs what sort of conversations take place in a boardroom and you'll hear the same thing: profit and loss, growth, productivity, commercial performance. We kid ourselves if we think that the boards concern themselves with the creative merit of a campaign or how many awards it could win. They just want to see marketing investment increase market share, minimise defection or drive numbers in some meaningful way."[25]

Unfortunately, Marc doesn't realise the crucial point – a lot of his adland peers would be appalled to sit in on such meetings. Not only are they not interested in "profit and loss, growth, productivity, and commercial performance", to many advertising folk such things are anathema.

And with that realisation, I believe we are getting to the heart of the matter. But before we explore that further, let's have one last explanation for why we've stopped selling.

It comes from Jonathan Bottomley, the former Chief Strategy Officer at Bartle Bogle Hegarty who believes "we have lost the ability to make what we make interesting".[26]

The skill shortage

If that's true then it's hardly surprising, is it? For, as I suggested above, we've abandoned the processes and practices that led to advertising that dramatised the benefit of the products/services we are supposed to be selling.

Not only do we not have the time for those processes and practices. We no longer understand their importance or have the skills to implement them.

Why? Because, as we all know, training sessions for members of staff were slashed during the post-financial crisis years of austerity, and have never been reinstated.

- Indeed, as far as in-house training is concerned, at most agencies you're as likely to get a lunchtime session on LGBTQ rights as a talk on how to write a brief or how to recognise – and have – a big idea.

Writing in the Bartle Bogle Hegarty blog, Lucian Trestler recommends we resurrect the old fashioned notion of "interrogating the thing to within an inch of its life, (so) it will reveal its true essence".[27] But, I am sure that such sound advice which originally came from BBH's founding partner, Nigel Bogle, would be pooh-poohed by many agency folk today.

And that's because, Trestler says, we no longer believe the product or service has a positive role to play in our prospects' lives. And when that happens we "resort to cramming messages into the first 5 seconds (quick before they skip) and let the digital platforms spam people's eyes with meaningless banners disguised as social posts."[28]

Does anyone care that no one will notice this work? That it's a sales opportunity that's been lost forever? I doubt it, because selling things is no longer our priority. Indeed, forget "priority". It isn't even on the list of things an agency does.

2
Why we've lost interest in selling

It wasn't always like this.

When I started in the industry, I was lucky enough to be taken on by Ogilvy & Mather Direct in London.

We were direct marketers, so our job was all about selling. That aim was shared by our advertising peers who made clients' brands famous, desirable – and, ultimately, buyable

All this was impressed upon us by our founder, David Ogilvy, who had "We Sell – or Else" emblazoned on the wall in every reception area in every Ogilvy office in the world.

Turning up for work each day, we knew what we were there to do.

But you will not find that four letter word on the agency's website today.

Indeed, look at the sites of the UK's top 10 agencies and you'll see no overt reference to their ability to – or intention of – selling anything to anyone.

The two mountaineers

Of course, the UK ad industry has always been a bit sniffy about selling things.

Most of those classic commercials of the '70s, '80s and '90s were aimed at raising awareness and never anything as vulgar as directly making the cash register ring.

But there'd been a general acknowledgement that advertising was ultimately about shifting products off shelves. And that adland had a symbiotic relationship with its clients that worked to their mutual benefit: they both made money.

As such, it was broadly accepted that advertising lubricated the machinery of the free market economy. Or, wildly mixing my metaphors, advertising and capitalism were roped together like two mountaineers – each reliant upon the other to keep climbing and avoiding those occasional quick and calamitous descents.

This mutual benefit was best seen in the relationship between the Conservative Party and Saatchi & Saatchi. The fact that the most creative, exciting, audacious agency in London could be so inextricably linked with Thatcherism must strike today's adlanders as not only incredible but also quite shameful.

Because things have changed. A haughty indifference to flogging stuff has become an open aversion; and a large percentage of the people who work in the industry want to cut the rope that binds them to capitalist enterprise. In fact, many would happily shove capitalism off the cliff.

Mark Ritson has recognised something similar on the client side.

As he said, the fact that "you could lose a marketing pitch because you wanted to make money shows ... how strangely detached from commercial reality our little profession has become in recent years." [1]

He went on to ask:

"Why is profit so uncool?"[2]

The answer is pretty simple: the pursuit of profit is what drives a business forward in a capitalist economy. No profit. No business.

Yet, for many ad people, profit is not only uncool, it is a dirty word.

Take, for example, this article "Milton Friedman was wrong", from *The Drum*.[3] Its author, Scott Goodson of Strawberry Frog, was commenting on the Nobel Prize winning economist's 1970 axiom that a company's only social responsibility is to its shareholders.

Now it's been accepted for some time that this is not a great idea. For example, Peter Drucker dismissed it in 1973. Then, writing in *Business Week* back in 1979, Quaker Oats president Kenneth Mason called Friedman's philosophy a "dreary and demeaning view of the role of business and business leaders in our society." And he went on to argue for the kind of time-honoured Quaker business ethics that we now call corporate social responsibility.[4]

But mention Milton to Goodson and he jumps, in one reflexive leap, to the blanket condemnation that, in the world of corporate business: "Profit is everything and Greed is good".[5]

Profit and Greed: the Tweedledum and Tweedledee of the liberal left's anti-capitalist narrative.

It's a story I first heard in my sixth form common room in the early 1970s. Back then it was told by a bunch of Hairies in army surplus greatcoats, a copy of *The Morning Star* in one hand and the latest Led Zep album in the other.

Today you hear it echoing down the industrially-lit, reclaimed-wood corridors of the UK's biggest, richest advertising, media and PR companies.

And, in this most globalised of industries, you'll find its

source in the corporate HQs of the network agencies based on the east and west coasts of the United States.

The Trump effect

Will Burns, a veteran of such great American shops as Goodby, Silverstein & Partners, and Weiden + Kennedy, described the situation in an article in *Forbes* magazine. He estimated that around 85–90% of advertising people were left-leaning liberals, and a good proportion of them were in Bernie Sanders's socialist camp in 2016.[6]

Even before Trump won that year's election, life was difficult for those who held opposing views.

Shareen Pathak, writing in *Digiday* in March 2016 observed: "For Republicans, it might be the hardest time to be part of an agency. In a bombshell election year, nothing is more isolating – or ostracizing – than being a conservative ... Over the course of dozens of interviews with multiple agency employees, a common thread emerged: The agency world is open as long as you stand for the 'right' things. And right now, being Republican is as wrong as it gets."[7]

The situation only got worse after the 2016 election.

As Burns pointed out: "I have personally noticed that my liberal-leaning advertising friends (which is nearly all of them) have become unhinged since Trump won. The vitriol with which they post their distaste for any Trump supporter and the speed with which they brand Trump supporters as automatic racists, misogynists, and xenophobes, has been alarming."[8]

Many expressed their anger in their creative work. At the 2017 Cannes Advertising Festival there were no fewer than 64 anti-Trump entries. As opposed to, well you can imagine how many anti-Hillary ads there were.[9]

She had a formidable array of talent on her side. Droga5, the best agency of the past ten years, signed up for Hillary. As did the best agency of the past 30 years, Goodby, Silverstein & Partners (GS&P).

I asked Derek Robson, the President of GS&P, what things were like now and he told me that, not surprisingly, conservatives tend to keep their views to themselves. "Generally," he continued, "the industry is predominantly left-leaning (almost embarrassingly one-sided for an industry that is meant to represent everyone).

"Our agency is almost totally left-leaning but I think it probably splits by age in terms of candidate. The younger folks are more likely to be in the Bernie camp (much more progressive). The older folks tend to be more pragmatic and therefore will probably vote for the candidate most likely to beat the Dorito-colored President."[10]

The left dominates in the UK as well

The UK advertising industry's left-wing tendency is apparent to anyone who works in a London-based agency. But, if in doubt, look at the research findings in *The Empathy Delusion* by Andrew Tenzer and Ian Murray.[11]

A quantitative survey questioned 199 marketing and advertising professionals. Alongside them were 2,019 UK citizens from the "modern mainstream" which is defined as the middle 50% in terms of household income (20k–55k) and represents over 50% of brand buyers across 3,500 brands.

The Empathy Delusion's research indicates that, politically, the "modern mainstream" identifies as 23% right, 52% centre and 25% left.

Conversely, the advertising and marketing community identifies as 20% right, 36% centre and 44% left.[12]

Which means that we who work in advertising and marketing are almost twice as likely to be left-leaning as the people we're supposed to be selling to.

We're the metropolitan bourgeoisie

That may not be as surprising as it sounds. As the 2019 general election indicated, politically the UK's tectonic plates have shifted. The Conservatives are now the most popular party amongst the working classes and Labour are the party of the primarily London-based, metropolitan bourgeoisie.

When it comes to the ad industry, it doesn't get much more metropolitan or bourgeois.

We are the most London-centric of industries. And pay wise, we are comfortably middle class.

According to the *Major Players Salary Survey* for 2019, those working in Digital, Creative and Tech have been relatively untouched by the business uncertainty surrounding Brexit. "Despite modest growth in the economy, there were still a significant number of pay rises across the board. Around 60% received a pay rise and 25% received a rise of over 10%."

Those working in Social and Content earn between £30,000 and £80,000; Creative and Design earn between £25,000 and £110,000, Design and Branding between £24,000 and £120,000.

And in Client Service, a graduate starts on £20,000 and can work their way up to Board Level where the basic is £100,000.[13]

So, most of us are bringing home more than the average Brit who gets around £29,558 a year. And substantially more than the poor buggers who work in the north. For example, Huddersfield and Wigan, where the average is £22,048 and £22,256 respectively.[14]

Here's more research to back that up

So, are we an industry of Champagne Socialists?

I asked Benedict Pringle who is the industry's expert on political advertising.

His impression is that the thought leaders probably are more committed to the Labour Party than the rank and file. The majority, he says, are definitely left-leaning but it is less an affiliation with the Labour Party and more an affinity with progressive liberal causes.

"For example, I was speaking to a group of people keen to get into the ad industry and was struck by the number who explained that whilst they were willing to work on a variety of categories, they really had their heart set on doing work for those brands who used their communications to have a broader social impact; it was as if they would have to hold their noses whilst doing anything commercial."[15]

I am aware that anecdotes are not data. And, thus far, I have only cited Tenzer and Murray's research. I also know that one statistical swallow doesn't make a substantive summer. So, in the weeks before the last general election, I did some polling of my own.

First I asked the marketing department of a large City-based company that sells financial investment services and energy supplies. Even here, in the belly of the capitalist beast, I found that 59% were either centre-left or left-wing.[16]

I got an almost identical result from attendees at a seminar I did at The Copy Club. Again I was surprised by the result because The Copy Club is: "A network of marketers in small or entrepreneurial businesses who get together in casual, fun settings; primarily a hub for small business owners who meet to swap ideas and share insights."[17]

Now you might expect these budding entrepreneurs to have been turned off by the anti-capitalist bent of Jeremy Corbyn and John McDonnell's Labour Party. But, no, fully 58.62% were centre-left/left, while 17.4% were centre-right/right and 24% were not sure/don't know.[18]

Moving to the agency world, I asked the same questions of the 2,000 employees at two advertising, digital and direct agencies from the same international network. The first was based 95 miles outside Central London: 49.87% were centre-left/left, 15.19% were centre-right/right and 35.44% were not sure/don't know.

Then I focused on that shop's sister agency in London, and here the metropolitan effect was marked with 67.97% centre-left/left, 13.74% centre-right/right and 18.30% not sure/don't know.[19]

So, according to my research, across clients, small business owners and agency personnel, advertising and marketing people on the left outnumber those on the right by over three or even four to one.

All of which confirms the findings of *The Empathy Delusion's* research and the conclusion that the advertising industry is overwhelmingly more left-wing than a sample of the general population would be.

Now let's set aside, for a moment, how this might affect our ability to understand or identify with our audience.

Instead, let's focus on how the left-leaning ad folk handle working in a system that many distrust, dislike and even despise.

From Blur to Corbyn

For them, being gainfully employed in an industry so associated with capitalism is, to say the very least, an embarrassment. Especially when they can be accused of creating the wants and needs that drive and perpetuate that system.

It was a lot easier during the Blair/Brown years. Back then, the Labour Party was a consensual, moderate, social democratic force with an economic policy based on centrist support for the free market.

As such, those who worked in advertising could do their own bit of triangulation, and see no real conflict between their Labour-voting credentials and their contribution to the great hog wallow of consumer capitalism.

But when Jeremy Corbyn became leader of the Labour Party, the consensus was rejected. Class war was declared and there was to be no fraternising with an enemy who were now "Tory scum" at best, and "murderers with blood on their hands" at worst.

In such an adversarial setting, it was increasingly difficult for advertising people to blur the edge between politics and profession. The days of peaceful co-existence had come to an abrupt end as left-leaning lurched over into angry condemnation of anything associated with the free market.

Jeremy may now have gone but Corbynism is still with us. So it can't be easy for any committed supporter to write strategies and create work for British Gas, Scottish Power, Thames Water, GNER or Avanti West Coast trains. After all, it's an article of faith that they be taken out of the private sector and returned to state ownership.

As for working on Lloyd's, RBS or Barclays, I imagine that, in a predominantly left-leaning creative department, the queue for those briefs will be only slightly shorter than those for the latest Shell and BP commercial.

"Wildly empathetic"

But maybe I'm worrying unduly about my peers allowing personal political bias to come before the task in hand.

After all, I'm sure they'll say they can set aside any personal issues and see the product/service they are advertising through the eyes of the people they are creating for.

In short, empathise with them.

Indeed, going back to the situation in the US, this is precisely the point made by Will Burns in the *Forbes* article I cited earlier. There he said: "Maybe there is a liberal bias in the ad world, but maybe it doesn't matter. Fact is, advertising people are not only creative, they are wildly empathetic. They have an incredible ability to put themselves into the shoes of their audience, no matter how different from them their audiences may be. It's part of the job."[20]

It's a nice, comforting thought. Alas, it is far from the truth – as the US industry admitted on the morning of November 9th, 2016 with the news of Donald Trump's election victory.

Once they'd got over the initial shock, industry leaders queued up to say how much they'd misjudged – or more accurately ignored – their 60 million countrymen who'd voted for the new president. And that this would mean a re-think of how future advertising was planned and executed.

McCann's CEO, Harris Diamond said "every so often you have to reset what is the aspirational goal the public has with regard to the products we sell. So many marketing programs are oriented towards metro elite imagery." Instead of reflecting the values of New York and Los Angeles, future ads would have to be more about "Des Moines and Scranton."[21]

Off to the jungle

Suddenly advertising's cosseted, corporate panjandrums were very keen to get out and meet "the people".

That this would be an expedition into the unknown is clear from a revealing metaphor employed by David Sable (then Global CEO of Y&R). "If you want to know how the lion hunts you don't go to the zoo, you go to the jungle."[22]

"Zoo"? "Jungle"? Who knows what wild and potentially dangerous creatures Mr Sable expected to encounter in his expedition west of Hoboken.

In reference to other descriptors of these exotic folk, agency chief, Paul Jankowski, said he'd heard agency and brand executives use "just about every stereotype out there: Rednecks, country bumpkins, dumb, bible beaters, overweight, proud of ignorance, intolerance . . ."

Writing in *Ad Age*, Jankowski continued: "What's most alarming is the fact that these comments are from people responsible for creating marketing campaigns. Their personal biases can affect an entire campaign's message, based on a lack of qualitative understanding of what makes the population segment tick. An innate, negative point of view has the effect of boxing out real insights."[23]

Tech reporter and prolific marketing blogger Patricio Robles believes the consequences could be dire. He warns that if brands entrust their marketing campaigns to agencies who cannot connect with or share the worldview of their customers then they "risk adopting strategies and campaigns that, at best, won't resonate with a large portion of the consumer population and, at worst, could alienate huge numbers of consumers."[24]

Robert Senior, who was then the Worldwide CEO of Saatchi and Saatchi, felt that agencies and brands would be too pragmatic to make such mistakes. He accepted the need for change and, after the Trump win, predicted that a different kind of advertising message would emerge. "The election will have spooked the liberal elite away from high concept 'make the world a better place' advertising to a more down-to-earth 'tell me what it will do for me' approach."[25]

As we'll see, Robert could not have been more wrong.

But before we look at the liberal elite's actual response, let's get back to empathy – and how the UK industry stacks up on that front.

3
Why our left-wing bias makes us so intolerant

Earlier, we saw the breakdown of the advertising and marketing community's political affiliations, and how our industry is widely left of centre compared to the mainstream.

Now you'd think that this heavy preponderance of people who generally pride themselves on their openness and tolerance would make the ad industry demonstrably more empathetic than the norm.

Especially given that we are professionals who sell ourselves on our ability to identify with target audiences whose lifestyles and needs are different from our own.

But, according to *The Empathy Delusion* research I referred to in the last chapter, that's just not true.

Representatives from the modern mainstream and the advertising and marketing industry were shown a series of statements devised by academic psychologists to determine levels of empathy.

The responses of both groups was almost identical, indicating that "people working in advertising and marketing have no special aptitude for understanding others ...This means we are no better at understanding other people's emotions and perspective than the mainstream."[1]

A question of morality?

The researchers decided more investigation was needed to explain these unexpected findings. And this meant delving into the morals and values of those who'd initially been questioned.

Now this is a tricky subject because upbringing, personality and life experiences all inform an individual's moral intuitions. However, social psychologists recognise five broad moral constructs found in all human relationships. These deal with: 1) Care or Harm, 2) Fairness or Cheating, 3) Loyalty or Betrayal, 4) Authority or Subversion, 5) Purity or Desecration.[2]

These five are the basis for Moral Foundations Theory and, as such, were the key to enabling social psychologist, Jonathan Haidt, to understand how morality determines our political opinions.[3]

A left-leaning democrat himself, Haidt's starting point was the conventional view that there was something wrong with conservatives or: "Why don't conservatives embrace equality, diversity, and change like normal people?"[4]

His research soon told him that this was, in fact, not the problem.

As Haidt explains in *The Righteous Mind,* attaching importance to diversity and equality is the natural response of those whose values rest on the care/harm and fairness/cheating foundations which he terms "Individualising". These foundations support ideals of social justice, compassion for the poor and the struggle for political equality.

Obviously, those on the left are big subscribers. But they don't have a monopoly.

The beliefs and behaviours of those on the right are also shaped by Individualising modes of thinking. The difference is that conservatives have a more complex and complete set of influences.

For Haidt pointed out that contemporary morality has three other equally important attributes. He gave these the umbrella term "Binding" and said they are focused on loyalty to the group, respect for authority and the ethics of community.

Tapping into conservative values

In his *Ad Age* article, cited above, Paul Jankowski shone a light on how important are those Binding values to conservative, Trump-voting consumers: "Core values such as faith (not religion), community and family are common threads that weave through a very diverse group of people."

He was equally clear about how important it was for marketers to acknowledge and respect such fundamental drivers of behaviour. "Understanding these core values as ways into a relationship, rather than divisive traits, will be vital to marketers in the post-election."[5]

Vital, but also extremely difficult. Because, as Haidt's research indicated, liberals (and by that I mean the vast majority of people in the US ad industry) do not relate to the ethical behaviour centred on loyalty, authority and community.

Indeed, he has found that many on the left "stayed locked into their Care-based moral matrices and refused to believe that conservatism was an alternative moral vision."[6]

As David Goodhart commented in the *Financial Times*: "It is as though conservatives can hear five octaves of music, but liberals respond to just two, within which they have become particularly discerning."[7]

If that is the case, then Paul Jankowski's appeal for understanding will probably fall on deaf ears.

The outliers of intolerance

Would the same situation obtain here in the UK? Well, the researchers working on *The Empathy Delusion* ran the same tests that Haidt had used for the US, and guess what?

The results were almost identical. People on the left discount the Binding ethics that inform the lives of those in the mainstream. But there was an added twist.

It emerged that those who work in marketing and advertising are even more dismissive of ethics based on loyalty, authority and community than those in the left-leaning mainstream.

As Andrew Tenzer and Ian Murray explained: "Crucially, in terms of moral foundations, people in our industry don't even connect fully with the political and ideological tribes they claim to connect with."[8]

The authors concluded: "There is a persistent belief in the industry that we have stronger empathy or that we are trained to overcome our biases. But it turns out we are more likely to be driven by these biases than the modern mainstream."[9]

Which is to say, because of our heavy left-wing leanings, we are less tolerant and more discriminatory.

Time to mention Brexit?

As in the US, agency colleagues who hold the "wrong" opinions can be the victims of this intolerance.

In the aftermath of the Brexit vote, Jeremy Bullmore, who many consider to be the wisest man in advertising, received a letter from one employee asking: "How do I stop a young female colleague who voted for Brexit from being bullied?"

The sage replied: "You're absolutely right to be concerned for your junior marketer. And it's going to get worse . . . Unless, that is, you remind your company that it is a fundamental requirement of marketing people to have an instinctive feel for their ultimate consumers. And, on the evidence of the referendum vote, the only member of your company to have such an understanding is this junior. It is the teasers and the bullies who should be made to feel inadequate: they continue to behave as members of that out-of-touch metropolitan elite against whom 17,410,742 members of the public – your consumers – decisively rebelled."

Another person wrote in and asked:"Do you agree that Brexit has exposed how out of touch advertising and media have become with regard to most places outside London? How should agencies respond to this?"

Jeremy responded: "Yes, I do. See above. And, as ever, greater diversity is part of the answer. But not just gender or ethnic diversity; diversity of prejudice is at least as important. How many people do you have in your agency who fully understood Nigel Farage and why getting on four million consumers voted for him? Opinion polls and focus groups help but they're not enough: you can't outsource empathy."[10]

We're beneviolent dictators

That was in 2016. As *The Empathy Delusion's* research cited below indicates, Jeremy's advice hasn't been followed.

A representative sample was asked to play The Dictator Game which was originally devised by Nobel Prize winning psychologist and economist, Daniel Kahneman and Richard Thaler and Jack Knetch. In this experiment, the subject was given £50 and asked what percentage they would share with another person.

It's heartwarming to know that 77% of modern mainstream offered to split the money 50-50. And it's slightly embarrassing to find that the people in advertising and marketing were less generous, with 69% giving away 25 quid.

But when the money was held by an ad person who voted Remain and they were asked to share with someone who held the same view on Brexit, some 82% agreed to share the dough.

However, when the game was played between someone who voted to Remain in the EU and someone who voted to Leave, only 42% of the Remainers were willing to share the money 50-50.

The authors of *The Empathy Delusion*, Andrew Tenzer and Ian Murray concluded: "This departure from the fairness norm is a clear sign of a tendency to punish or discriminate against those holding opposing beliefs."[11]

So this evidence suggests that those who self-identify as being on the left can exhibit a capacity for intolerance that borders on the vindictive.

There are no figures for how those who voted to Leave would have shared the money with a Remain partner. So, to compare the tolerance levels of the supporters of each faction, let's turn to the polls conducted by YouGov in August 2019.

Not in the family

A sample of Remain and Leave voters was asked: "How would you feel if you had a son or a daughter who married someone who held the opposite opinion?"

Remain supporters tend to argue that they're backing the side that stands for diversity and tolerance. And yet 39% of them said they would be upset if their son or daughter married a Leave voter.

As for the people who have often been dubbed prejudiced bigots by their detractors, just 11% of those who voted Leave would object to having a Remainer in the family.[12]

A similar picture emerged when the same question was asked of those who support the Conservative and Labour parties.

Just 13% of Conservative parents said they would feel upset about having a Labour voting daughter or son-in-law.

But 34% of Labour parents said they would feel that way if they had a Conservative daughter or son-in-law.[13]

Not that such couplings are likely, for the same intolerance is evident on many of the popular dating apps.

Conservative journalist Charlotte Gill found open hostility, with a typical profile reading: "I get along best with people who can check their privilege and hate the Tories." Another woman described herself as valuing "kindness and compassion" yet added "f*** the Tories" in her self-summary box.[14]

The journalist experienced the same discrimination when flat hunting on SpareRoom.com. While no one on the right seemed averse to sharing with Labour voters, it appears that the old "No Irish, no blacks, no dogs" exclusions have been replaced by "No Tories. No Brexiteers". Nowadays the liberal left's commitment to diversity only extends to the dogs.[15]

Equal opportunity intolerance

If such prejudice surprises you, it isn't news to psychologists and social scientists.

Research that was presented to the Society of Personality and Social Psychology backs up both Jonathan Haidt's findings and those indicated by the YouGov polls. Indeed, it confirms that conservatives, liberals, the religious and the non-religious are equally prejudiced. As Matthew Hutson summarises in the admirably impartial *Politico* magazine: "While liberals might like to think of themselves as more open-minded, they are no more tolerant of people unlike them than their conservative counterparts are."[16]

This conclusion has been supported by numerous similar studies.

For example, the American psychologist, Mark Brandt, addressed the issue in *The Ideological-Conflict Hypothesis: Intolerance Among Both Liberals and Conservatives*. He concluded that, despite the liberals' attachment to universalism, they and their conservative counterparts "express similar levels of intolerance toward ideologically dissimilar and threatening groups."[17]

Brandt's findings have been corroborated by research conducted at St Louis University and The College of New Jersey and "both have also found approximately equal prejudice among conservatives and liberals."[18]

Finally, in October 2019, the *American Political Science Review* – one of the alpha journals of US political science – published a paper describing the toxic effects of what it termed "affective polarisation".

In essence, regardless of your left/right leanings, the more favourably you rate the political party that you endorse (the ingroup) the lower you rate the opposition (the outgroup).[19]

So, the downside of passionate commitment is often violent loathing. For evidence of this, just look at the posts from people who regularly share their political views on social media.

Or ask Claire Beale, the editor of *Campaign* magazine.

Adland's angry echo chambers

In her July 2019 *Love and Hate* issue, Claire decided to conduct an interview with the leader of the Brexit Party, Nigel Farage. She also opted to put his photograph on the cover.[20]

Now, in her long and successful career at *Campaign,* Claire has been both a great role model for females in our industry and a champion of diversity. But this counted for nothing in the hours after the interview appeared.

In the ensuing social media storm, she was subjected to personal and professional attacks for giving a "fascist" a "bigot" and a "racist" such publicity. This despite the fact that the politician her detractors wanted silenced had launched the Brexit Party brand only six months earlier and garnered 39% of the popular vote in the recently contested European elections.

Of course, such popular support meant nothing to Farage's detractors because, to borrow the term Mark Brandt used above, his supporters were "ideologically dissimilar and threatening" to them.

Thus threatened, these outraged liberals sprayed the slurry of abuse all over Twitter and Facebook in an effort to shut down any further debate. It's an old trick: accuse your opponent of being a "fascist" or a "racist" (or, for that matter, an "anti-Semite"), and you've essentially ring fenced their opinions and marked them unworthy of discussion.

Such a discussion about Farage might have led them to the uncomfortable truth that he had managed what they seem incapable of doing. And that is empathise with the people outside the bubble in which they live. Not only that, he had built a very distinctive positioning for his brand based upon that insight and understanding.

As the multi-award-winning copywriter, Paul Burke, observed: "You'd think they might want to learn from someone who's done these things so recently, quickly and successfully. But you'd be wrong."[21]

From the bottom to the very top

Apart from Paul, myself and Dave Trott, few industry people defended Claire and the principle of free speech.

Understandably so, because who would want to be on the receiving end of the bile being aimed at her?

Now it might be comforting to think that such abuse comes from a few hyper-aggressive individuals from the far reaches of the hard left.

But I'm afraid not. It is all pervasive. And comes from the very top.

Take for example, D&AD, the advertising world's most influential, important and respected industry body.

The role of CEO of D&AD comes with prestige and responsibility, and whoever holds that position speaks with all the authority and influence associated with this august institution.

So, what did D&AD's CEO tweet on May 29th, 2019?

"Matt Hancock on *Newsnight*? Drunk, stupid or just representative of the general Tory leadership candidate standard? What a complete c**t."[22]

This, I hasten to add, is Tim Lindsay's private Twitter account. But, in the handful of words that Twitter allow you to say who you are and why you're worth following, he advertises himself as "CEO of D&AD". And, since he's chosen not to have an official D&AD account (I suggested he open one two years ago), he uses it to communicate his news of what is happening at the organisation he represents.

However, interspersed with messages about D&AD, are his views on what is happening at Westminster. Suffice to say, in the six months after the above tweet appeared, the latter items far outnumbered the former. And many were, to put it politely, good examples of the blind antipathy toward the "outgroup" that's brought on by "affective polarisation".*

---

* *In December 2020, Tim changed his descriptor to "Old adman".*

4
Why we're saving the world

This class war banter is all well and good while we're talking amongst ourselves at work. And we can enliven it by having a moan about the big, bad corporate clients we're working for.

Indeed, a lot of us are the employees of big, bad corporations ourselves, which means we can bitch about our bosses as well.

But perhaps we're being a tad disingenuous when we do this because anyone working for the big multinational advertising networks has already removed themselves from the free market. Indeed, the big publicly listed corporations are enclaves of socialism within the enterprise economy.

Their bigness protects them from the competition and downturns that can quickly drive an independent to the wall.

Their bureaucracies support the mediocre, and allow failures to be moved sideways into sinecures somewhere else in the organisation.

And perhaps most importantly, their expense-account funded, graduate-to-retirement jobs offer many of their employees the kind of security that only the networks' quasi-statist, corporate welfare can afford.

This is what advertising does now

Like I say, reinforcing each other's contempt for the networks and spending a few hours on Facebook doing virtual fist bumps with those we agree with gets us through the working day.

But how about the evening? What happens when we meet up with our friends – the ones who don't work in the industry and who don't understand that we're a sleeper cell secretly subverting the system from within?

These people want to know why we're still working as a capitalist running dog.

And it's at this point we explain that, in actual fact, advertising no longer has anything to do with furthering the free market. This is, after all, not the 1980s.

It's 2020 and we gave up selling things long ago.

We are, instead, on a mission to save the planet and alert its inhabitants to the evils of climate change, privilege, racism, cultural appropriation, and whatever might constitute a #MeToo or LGBTQIA infraction.

This is what advertising does now.

Brands are no longer to be promoted on the fact that they clean your whites whiter, but on their power to make your conscience cleaner. Being a force for good is the new purpose of brands and those who market them to the public

In short, adland has at last discovered its righteous raison d'etre.

The pioneers of purpose

I say "at last" but actually the social purpose movement has been gathering momentum for over a decade.

Its manifesto was written by Scott Goodson of Strawberry Frog, David Jones who was at that time CEO of Havas, and Jim Stengel, the ex-CMO of P&G.[1]

All the endangered planets must have been aligned in 2012, because, in that year, those three launched their books in the UK:

Goodson: *Uprising: How to build a brand - and change the world - by sparking cultural movements.*

Jones: *Who cares wins: Why good business is better business.*

Stengel: *Grow: How ideals power growth and profit for the world's greatest companies.*

From then on the social purpose movement was up and running. And, given the potential it held for promoting their own progressive causes, left-leaning adfolk once more started looking forward to writing strategies and doing some creative.

D&AD and Cannes

Their enthusiasm surged when the two big global advertising competitions, D&AD and Cannes, announced they'd be giving awards for ads aimed: "at changing the world for the better". [2]

Cannes trumped its rival in June 2012 with the "Chimera Project" which was launched by former US President, Bill Clinton. In his keynote speech, he urged the advertising industry to use its "formidable powers of communication and persuasion" to solve the world's most pressing problems which he listed as "climate change, gender equality, and personal empowerment."[3]

Since then, the social justice alliance he was championing has expanded to include #MeToo and Time's Up. And you can't help but wonder if today's members would be quite so happy to give a platform to old Slick Willie. Remember Monica Lewinsky?

But back to 2012 and, in November of that month, D&AD announced its White Pencil Symposium – "A conversation about the power of commercial creativity to make our world a better place."[4]

Today, D&AD calls the White Pencil "the ultimate accolade for creative work that makes a real difference."[5]

Cannes's organisers would disagree. Virtually every Lion they hand out now has some connection to social purpose. And that includes 16 of this year's 21 Grand Prix winners.[6] As *Adweek* said: "Social responsibility was once actually a category at Cannes, but this year marked the first at which it wasn't. The theme is now so ubiquitous throughout all the best creative work and award winners that it no longer needs a category."[7]

It is "ubiquitous" because creatives know they've little chance of winning a Lion unless they submit a purpose-driven piece. Carol Cone, a pioneer of social impact campaigns, spelled it out to them: "In a large part the judges are prioritizing meaningful work: judges from the Outdoor, Entertainment, Design, Press, and PR juries all spoke about the importance of work that has a positive effect on the world".[8]

She says "prioritising", but she really means that those judges are forcing their agenda upon the global creative community. Or to put it another way, they're playing their own version of Daniel Kahneman's Dictator Game. Generous with those who share their views, but penalising those who don't.

In short, they are enforcing a sanctimonious, woke orthodoxy in an industry that thrives on irreverent, creative freedom.

And the consequences of that? Well, here's one of advertising's smartest thinkers, Saatchi & Saatchi's Richard Huntington on the dangers of groupthink: "A visceral loathing of orthodoxy ought to be the key qualification in getting a job in advertising or marketing. Those that take comfort from the accepted wisdom of others are ill-prepared to face the future challenges of our brands and businesses."[9]

Sorry James, no one's interested

So what then of the business of selling? Or, for that matter, the selling of business?

Well, let's take a detour here and look at *Long may we "rain"* – a film produced for the 2019 Cannes Festival by the Department of International Trade and its partners in the UK media industry.

At its conclusion James Murphy, founder of the hugely successful Adam & Eve agency, tells the audience "what we have effectively is a Creative Team GB. It's the beginning of a three-year programme and it's a programme that really is there to deliver a 'Buccaneering Brexit'. Showing the world that we're open for business, and we've got global talent that can project its abilities all around the world."[10]

I say he "tells his audience" but actually, amongst his peers in the advertising industry, there isn't an audience for such an enterprise-oriented message. Especially one that mentions Brexit as an opportunity. More than seven months after the film was posted, it's had 306 views.

And no comments.

However, James's journey to Cannes wasn't wasted. While there he took part in another film. This time he was one of six advertising luminaries asked by *Campaign* magazine to summarise British creativity in one sentence. Of those six, two took the party line and highlighted how "diverse" we are, despite the fact that, well, we'll get to that later.

As to admiring work that sells? When asked to name their favourite piece of UK creative, James was one of only two who cited ads aimed at actually shifting product – his former agency's excellent Marmite campaign, by the way. Predictably, the other four of the six voted for work with a social purpose.[11]

Viva la Vulva

One of their favourites was *Viva la Vulva*. In fact, at Cannes, everyone loved it.

The final night of the Festival was given over to the Glass Lion for Change where *Viva la Vulva* won Gold for work that "truly made a difference" and where "marketing helped change the world".[12]

I'm sure you know all about *Viva la Vulva* but, if not, then it is designed to fight "the myths, insecurities and stereotypes that women are subjected to when it comes to their genitals."[13]

In the film, those genitals are variously represented by a singing clam, a half a mango, an oyster on the shell, an open purse, a sliced lemon etc.

It's all stylishly, expensively and entertainingly done, and looks, for all the world, like a great pop video. But it is worth noting that it is "stylishly, expensively and entertainingly done" *by men*. As Patrick Collister points out in his *Cannes Conflicted* report, not one of the eight creatives credited for *Viva la Vulva* was female.[14] Which means the project itself exemplifies all the "ingrained gender inequality, imbalance or injustice" that the Glass Lion seeks to "positively impact".[15]

As for "truly making a difference" and "helping change the world", here are the results that the agency submitted to the Caples Awards – one of the few competitions that still asks for proof that the creative has worked:

"The bull's eye target for the campaign was Libresse's usual audience, women 18–39 years old, aiming at becoming relevant to them any time of the month (beyond five days). The campaign reached 90% of the target audience with engagement levels three times higher than the previous product-led campaign and the lowest CPM for all platforms. The long film was aimed at a wider audience through earned media, to change attitudes and open conversations at scale.

"Prominent opinion leaders have voiced their praise, and women everywhere have voiced their thanks.

"As Caitlin Moran tweeted: 'I might even buy A SECOND FANNY, in celebration'."[16]

So, was this "truly making a difference" and "helping change the world"?

On this, I defer to Tom Callaghan's view. Tom worked as a Creative Group Head (a Creative Director in today's money) during Saatchi & Saatchi's glory days, and is now a best-selling crime novelist. Whilst out of our racket, he is still a highly perceptive judge of creative:

"The film is aimed at its existing market, women who are not ashamed about having periods, whose family don't shun them or make them sleep in a separate hut when they're menstruating (as in Nepal), or for whom the family budget simply doesn't run to such 'luxuries'.

"Libresse needs growth – however much current users like the product, they're not going to buy more than they need. So growth and sales must surely come from emerging markets. This spot doesn't do anything to convince Third World women that the product will benefit them during their 'dirty time'.

"But hey, it won a Gold so everybody's happy. Except perhaps for the woman rinsing last month's bloody rag in the river so she can use it next time."[17]

Tom didn't bother mentioning the obvious fact that *Viva La Vulva* would never be shown in the conservative Third World countries where Libresse *could* make a difference. Indeed, it would be regarded as deeply offensive by the very people it was seeking to reassure.

Not all good causes are worthy

Maybe agencies and juries will get round to considering these women next year. But I doubt it, because, just like a product, each purpose appears to have a limited shelf life. And the choice of subject matter seems dictated by what is trending, and most likely to play on the judges' consciousness and consciences.

For example, in *Cannes Conflicted*, Patrick Collister points out that the 2016 news headlines were dominated by the refugee crisis. Consequently, the following year at Cannes there were 63 refugee-related entries and a multi-Lion winner in the "Refugee Nation" work.

In 2018, there were 32 pieces of work on this subject. But no big winners.

So, having adopted the issue and got onto the awards shortlist, its advocates moved on. To the extent that in 2019, the refugees languished in their camps in Libya ignored by the EU who'd broken its promise to take in quotas – and by the ad industry who, with just one exception, had moved on to the next big thing.[18]

At least the refugees got noticed in 2017 and '18.

Tibet's Buddhists, China's Uighur Muslims and Iraq's Christians are being persecuted to the point of extinction. And drawing attention to and helping alleviate their suffering would "truly make a difference" and be worthy of a Glass Lion.

But social justice warriors tend not to fight for religious causes. Reverence for Mosque, Temple and Church unites those conservatives who are influenced by

Jonathan Haidt's Bindings ethics. As such, liberals see these people as an obstacle on the road to their progressive utopia. Which is why no one rushes to their defence when they're being imprisoned and murdered – and why adland looks away.

Likewise, it's unlikely the demonstrators in Hong Kong will be getting much of a look in come June 2020. Defending democracy in Asia's hub of free market capitalism against a communist regime just isn't, well, where it's at. So, we won't be seeing many ad campaigns supporting them either.

No, adland's crusaders (can I still use that word?) will be sticking closely to the liberal progressive agenda.

And the winner is ... XR

Which means there are no prizes for guessing the hot topic at 2020's awards show. Extinction Rebellion's protests at last year's event guaranteed that.*

There are two good reasons they turned up at the festival.

First, air travel to Cannes – and the thousands of tonnes of CO_2 it creates – is difficult to justify. The town itself is pretty charmless and horribly expensive. In the past, I only went to pick up awards or judge them. (Today, the one thing that might tempt me back would be news that Ricky Gervais was MCing.)

Those UK delegates who justify their presence by

---

* 2020 was cancelled. In 2021 XR will doubtless be displaced by BLM.

saying it's a great place to hear new thoughts and expose themselves to different opinions and ideas would be better off spending four days talking to people in Blackpool, Wolverhampton or Swindon. That really would open their minds.

Secondly, XR were there because they equate advertising with capitalism which, in turn, they equate with consumption. And they are against all three.

Actually I'll row back on that. They probably didn't need to be making that point at Cannes because a lot of the attendees already agree with them.

Preaching to the choir

Laura Jordan Bambach, the founder of the agency Mr President and herself a former President of D&AD, saw their talk at The Drum Arms and felt it "so powerful it sucked the air out of the room."[19]

In her article in *The Drum*, she posed the question "Can Cannes Save the World?" and as a first step gave this rallying cry to her industry peers: "We're all in this together and I'd challenge you all to get Extinction Rebellion in to speak in your agency – they're easy to reach out to."

By then XR had already been in touch with the ad industry via an open letter that put the blame firmly at our door: "One of the reasons we've got here is because you've been selling things to people that they don't need. You are the manipulators and architects of that consumerist frenzy".[20]

They were preaching to the choir. Indeed, many XR activists used to be choristers themselves with insiders saying that a hard core of its leaders are from the marketing and advertising industry.

In an instant, 20 agencies pledged to avoid working on fossil fuel briefs and the IPA organised a sold-out climate crisis meeting of its 44 Club.[21]

By September, most of the agency world seemed ready to support Greta Thunberg's Climate Strike with over 80 agencies including Ogilvy, BBH, W+K, Cheil, Lucky Generals, Iris and TBWA all actively supporting the protest.[22]

Hundreds of agency staff met at Tate Britain in a show of solidarity. Given that China released more CO2 and methane last year than the US, EU and Japan combined, it might have made more sense to march on the embassy of the Peoples' Republic.[23]

They headed straight for Parliament Square instead. Interestingly, they were accompanied by those carrying *Socialist Worker* placards proclaiming "System Change – not Climate Change".[24]

I'm sure many agency folk on the march endorsed that sentiment. But if so, did they have any real idea what system XR would introduce to replace the capitalism that many of them despise?

And what would be the role of advertising in the post-capitalist, post-industrial world that they'd be helping to usher in?

Organically-fed turkeys and Christmas

The answer would be none at all. Even those agencies that believe they'll get a pass because they are working for clients with sustainability at their core are in for a nasty surprise.

Ian Christie, Ben Gallant and Simon Mair of the University of Surrey explain why in their article: "The Delusion of Boundless Economic Growth."

"Sustainable growth is a bad bet. The odds of success are bad. For sustainable growth we have to escape the limits of the Earth or decouple absolutely from negative externalities ... Sustainable growth offers us more of the same. More stuff, not more meaning and control."[25]

As they say, there are only two ways to have our sustainable cake and eat it. And that is for man to colonise a passing asteroid.

Or for resource efficiencies to increase at least as fast as economic output does, and to continue to improve as the economy grows. Such absolute decoupling is, in their opinion, almost as unlikely as us strip-mining the Moon.

The fundamental position for XR thinkers is: you cannot have limitless growth on a finite planet. Indeed, any kind of growth drives energy demand up, thus making it impossible to decarbonise the economy.

Degrowth

What they are proposing is localistic, post-industrial, communal, Malthusianism ushered in by degrowth. This would necessitate a programme of demand *reduction* – which is the opposite of what advertising is traditionally supposed to do.

This point has obviously occurred to David Gamble, Executive Creative Director of Truant London. As he told *Campaign* magazine: "To halve emissions in five to 10 years, we will need to unsell everything we've sold and been sold for the past 60 years. We'd have to unsell society as we know it. Unsell Christmas, unsell greed, unsell what success really looks like. But we would need to do it in a way that benefited people, rather than punished them or stripping away their lives and culture."[26]

According to Christie, Gallant and Mair, to achieve that last bit would mean focusing on: "Providing things that make life worth living beyond new consumer goods. More time with your family, more creative work, a more equitable distribution of income."[27]

There might well be time for "more creative work" but it won't be the kind that's done by anyone in an agency's creative department. In fact, if you currently work in advertising then, in a de-carbon, degrowth economy, you'll be about as employable as a chimney sweep.

And, according to the admirably clear-sighted left-leaning Canadian journalist, Leigh Phillips, so would everyone else. "Degrowth unwittingly endorses what would be an imposition of austerity on the Western working classes far beyond anything a Thatcher, Cameron or May could imagine, this time in the name of the planet.

"And worst of all, degrowth would bring an end to progress itself – the steady expansion of freedom for all humanity."[28]

And on that bleak and vatic note, I end this digression into the economic consequences of XR.

I took us there to point out the possible outcome of our industry's alliance with XR. And, through that association, to show just how extremely anti-capitalist the politics of adland have become.

So are we left-wing idealists or useful idiots? Bit of both, I suspect.

When it comes to our clients, however, there's a fair bit of idiocy on display but precious little idealism.

5
Why clients are embracing purpose

Certainly, clients are embracing social purpose – but not for the same politically and culturally charged reasons as their agency peers.

They see that's where future profits lie. And they're pursuing them ruthlessly.

Alan Jope, the CEO of Unilever, stood up at Cannes this summer and announced: "We will dispose of brands that we feel are not able to stand for something more important than making your hair shiny, your skin soft, your clothes whiter or your food tastier."

He said that's where the money was – with over half of Unilever's turnover coming from brands that he'd define as "purpose-led". It was a figure he foresaw soon rising to 80%, given that those purpose-driven brands were the company's fastest-growing assets.[1]

He is not alone.

In the UK, clients have taken to purpose with much the same zeal as they embraced CRM, social media, native advertising, influencer marketing and Big Data. And for the same reasons – they are looking for the marketing miracle that saves their ass.

Early stimulus

Their original enthusiasm was fired by Jim Stengel's aforementioned book *Grow*. On its first page, the former CMO at P&G revealed that "the data from a ten-year growth study of more than 50,000 brands around the world shows that companies with ideals of improving people's lives outperform the market by a huge margin

... those that embrace that fact are the ones that dominate their categories, create new categories and maximise profit in the long term."[2]

Everyone got very excited about this.

But then Richard Shotton rather spoiled things with his clinical dismantling of the argument in his 2018 book, *The Choice Factory.*

According to him, a lot of the companies Stengel listed did not have a share price, so his claim that they'd outperformed the market was bogus. Moreover, in the five years after the publication of Stengel's book only nine outperformed the S&P 500 benchmark.

Most tellingly, Shotton showed that Stengel had made no attempt to start with 50 companies that had a purpose and then work out if they'd been successful. Instead, Stengel skewed the data by choosing the 50 best performing brands from Millward Brown's 50,000 strong database.

After which, he went in search of the "ideals of improving people's lives" that lay at their core. And here, the truth is that a lot of the brands he cited had a purpose that was far from world changing. For example, Mercedes "exists to epitomise a life of achievement" or Moet & Chandon "exists to transform occasions into celebrations."

As Shotton concludes "because advertisers fervently hoped that the theory was true, they forgot to check whether it was. They have succumbed to a collective bout of wishful thinking".[3]

Accenture and P&G provide the proof

But that hasn't stopped them believing. And why not? There have been some very persuasive sound bites and stats to justify their faith. Those most often cited come direct from the Accenture Strategy Research Report: *To Affinity and Beyond. From Me to We – The Rise of the Purpose-Led Brand.*

For example, its survey of nearly 30,000 consumers in 35 countries – including more than 2,000 consumers in the United States – found that 62% of them wanted companies to take a clear position on current and broadly relevant issues such as sustainability, transparency and fair employment practices.

Closer to home, over half of UK consumers (53%) said they preferred to buy goods and services from companies that stand for a shared purpose that reflects their personal values and beliefs.[4]

That's pretty categoric. Then there was this from P&G.

In July 2019, *Forbes* magazine reported on how that company's "relentlessly disciplined consumer centric approach" was now focussed on the commercial potential of social purpose.[5]

The article then quoted Marc Pritchard, P&G's Chief Brand Officer: "Nine out of 10 people say they have a more positive image of a company when it supports social or environmental causes, and half say they make purchase decisions based on shared beliefs with the brand. And we have evidence from multiple brands, that those that are not only delivering superior performing products and packaging and advertising campaigns but are also doing good – they tend to grow more. And so it's good for business and it's good for the world."[6]

Impressive stuff. But bear in mind that this is the same P&G that sank billions into the digital delusion. And the same Marc Pritchard who, as we saw earlier, has spent the past four years correcting the damage and, in the process, firing 80% of his agencies.

Speaking of the digital delusion, this is from the influential Accenture Strategy Report I mentioned above. It reckons that with a purpose-driven strategy: "US companies have the opportunity to create a community of loyal, engaged and valuable brand stakeholders—all working together to usher in the next era of engagement and competitiveness".[7]

Which all sounds ominously like the promises made about digital's interactive potential fifteen years ago. And I'm afraid we all know what happened to those virtual communities, don't we?

Sustainable brands are growing faster …

But back to business and Marc Pritchard's view that social purpose can now be "a force for good and a force for growth".[8]

His rivals at Unilever are having similar success. During his speech at the Cannes Festival, CEO Alan Jope said that 28 of its sustainable brands grew 69% faster than the rest of the business in 2018, compared with 47% in 2017.[9]

It's easy to see why they are popular.

Here in the UK, consumers are happy to enjoy the benefits of globalisation and the free market but are also troubled by their shortcomings. *The Times's* columnist Caitlin Moran summed up their dilemma: "Think that unfettered capitalism might be out of control, but still like 'stuff'? Feel guilty about working conditions for employees ... but still like buying 'stuff'? Want to be a more considerate customer but still really, really like buying 'stuff'?"[10]

Those who share Moran's angst are aware that their liking for "stuff" is seriously damaging the environment. Incidentally, when it comes to saving the planet, these people are inspired not so much by a 17-year-old Swedish activist but by a 93-year-old English naturalist. Heeding David Attenborough's warnings, most accept they must do their bit.

So they'll be impressed to learn that Knorr is willing to invest up to one million euros a year supporting sustainably-grown food. Likewise, they'll think it's good of Persil to give handy hints on how to wash their clothes the environmentally friendly way. And it's admirable of Lipton's to team up with the Rainforest Alliance to conserve biodiversity and ensure a fair deal for all their workers.[11]

All these actions are likely to endear the brands to their customers. Indeed, they may well influence purchase choices.

... but their appeal might be limited

However, we should bear in mind that a successful media figure like Caitlin Moran, who I quoted above, is relatively rich. Which means she can indulge her penchant for more "stuff" and also shop around for the sustainable "stuff" that assuages her guilt. The majority of people can't afford either option – and have more pressing priorities.

For example, here in the UK, it's estimated that around 40% of all food shopping is bought to take advantage of a promotion of some kind.[12]

If you look at the eye-opening US report *What Science Says About Discounts, Promotions, and Free Offers* you'll also see that money-off coupons are driving e-commerce. Apparently, 62% of consumers invest two or more hours each week scouring the web for promotions. And two thirds "say they made a purchase they weren't originally planning to make solely based on finding a coupon or discount."[13]

In short, for a lot of people, saving the world is secondary to saving a few bob.

Moreover, the majority might be aware of the problems of globalisation and how it is damaging the planet. And they may well cite these in focus groups when asked about their brand preferences. But they have other preoccupations that they don't mention.

As Bob Hoffmann points out: "The average consumer has other things on her mind. Like why she gained two pounds last week, and why her father is looking pale, and why the fucking computer keeps losing its WiFi signal, and why Timmy's teacher wants to see her next week, and what's that bump she noticed on her arm."[14]

So, while we in adland get excited about sustainability we should, to paraphrase David Ogilvy, remember that: "The consumer isn't a vegan, she's your wife."

As such, it might be wise to present the good works done by Knorr, Persil and Lipton's as secondary and supporting reasons why the consumer should buy them.

This point is made by Richard Shotton, the man who we've just seen tearing Jim Stengel's argument to shreds: "Purpose can be valuable but should it be the focus of your marketing, do people really care about it when they are buying a burger or a soft drink or a pair of shoes? It is a long way from a primary motivator. The danger is that people think it is much more important due to a superficial look at survey data."[15]

A cautionary tale

Patrick Collister gives us hard evidence to support this view. In *Cannes Conflicted* he says that VW should now be a dead brand, its factories closed, the owners of its cars too ashamed to take them out of the garage.[16]

The reason being the car giant's admission, in 2015, that it had cheated carbon dioxide emissions tests in the US and that its engines had emitted nitrogen oxide pollutants up to 40 times above that allowed. According to VW some 11 million cars worldwide were affected.[17]

If the proponents of social purpose in business are to

be believed, that should have been the end of the road for VW. But what actually happened?

Headlines like this: "Volkswagen Profit Roars Back Two Years After Dieselgate".[18]

The article went on to say: "The world's largest carmaker, Volkswagen appeared to be back in racing form Friday, as its 2017 results revved back to levels not seen since its devastating 'dieselgate' emissions cheating scandal.

"VW said in a statement it had booked an 11.4 billion euros bottom line this year, more than double the 5.1 billion euros earned last year ... Record sales of some 10.74 million vehicles worldwide helped the group based in Wolfsburg, Germany to boost revenues 6.2% year-on-year."[19]

The car giant that should have died, continues in rude health, with first half year figures for 2019 showing booming sales and revenues.[20]

Such numbers do seem to have driven a hole in Unilever's belief that: "Business growth should not be at the expense of people and the planet".[21]

But wait, Unilever are definitely not alone in thinking this. Forget those car buyers who are happy to forgive VW's act of criminal environmental vandalism.

And disregard those cynics who like to rhyme "woke" with "broke".

There are two very distinct and lucrative markets for those brands that address ethical issues and social, environmental and cultural problems.

Let's meet them.

6
Who's buying the purpose pitch?

The obvious answer is the millennials.

According to the Chartered Institute of Marketing (CIM) survey of consumers aged 18- to 34-years-old:

81% of millennials would like companies to publicly commit to Corporate Social Responsibility values.

92% of millennials would choose to buy from a company committed to ethical business practices.

64% of millennial females bought, in the past year, a cause-related product.

82% of millennials would strive to be employed by a company recognised for its commitment to business ethics.

More than nine out of ten millennials would change brands to a cause-related one.[1]

It's no wonder they are susceptible to purpose-driven marketing. From nursery school onwards, they've been taught to consume such messages.

Every social purpose marketer's dream.

Here's Boaz Shoshan, Editor of *Capital and Conflict* describing his early woke awakening. "Older folks will recognise the three r's to mean reading, 'riting, and 'rithmetic ... I only learned about 'em a couple months back. You see, I was taught a *different* three r's at school. Mine all actually start with r: reduce, reuse, recycle.

"All through my education, beginning very early on, were constant signposts to an impending problem of climate change and environmental deterioration. The most blatant of these occurred when I was in primary school, when we were taken out of class for a cinema outing to watch Al Gore's . . . Oscar-winning documentary *An Inconvenient Truth*. Bear in mind, this was a state school. If memory serves, I don't even think my parents were asked to pay for the viewing."[2]

Nearly one in three of Boaz's peers headed off to University where their lecturers continued their indoctrination. You get some idea of the ideology they've been exposed to from the *Times Higher Education* survey's findings of December 2019. Apparently only 8% of academics said they'd be voting Conservative in that month's general election. The rest were firmly in the liberal/left camp.[3]

Not only have these tutors schooled their students in an orthodoxy that makes them feel guilty about the first world privileges they enjoy. The youngsters are also told they won't be enjoying those privileges for very much longer.

The millennial generation are the first since the Second World War who'll be worse off than their predecessors.[4] Not for them the expectations of material progress their elders might have known.

Nor, for that matter, their parents' slightly more balanced world view.

For the lack of ideological diversity that results from their tutors' bias is exacerbated by their activist colleagues who've turned the Students' Union into a Marxist madrasa and de-platformed, harassed and barracked those whose views they find objectionable.[5]

In short, they've emerged as every social purpose marketer's dream.

This is especially so, given that the woke sensibility appears to be a global phenomenon. Gianluca di Tondo, Heineken's Global Senior Brand Director, has been quite frank about how he's exploited it.

"Millennials make my life easier"

"I've been doing marketing for 20 years and for the first time I have an audience that is completely different from previous ones and they make my life easier. The notion of purpose has emerged everywhere, including in developing markets which we were not expecting. Usually you have cultural difference in developed and developing markets but today millennials are very similar. If you live in Nigeria or the US, this layer of stress is the same.

"It's easier to find a common denominator across them. In the past, I had to give 50/50 global/local. Today, in most of the markets, I can go 80/20. If you crack global insight well you only need a bit of localisation that digital will make simple."[6]

Di Tondo is certainly not alone in mining this rich seam. But there are those who see the roof falling in.

Mark Ritson has been ruthlessly critical of the blanket generalisations inherent in this mass market strategy.

"Even if the bullshit about millennials is true, what, as a marketer, are you going to do with it? Remember how you were trained to avoid mass marketing and to reject broad assumptions about the market? Well, what do you think millennials are? The minute marketers start thinking all millennials are the same, they reject the behavioural and attitudinal nuances of a hugely heterogeneous population and collapse them into one big, generic mess.

"If you buy the idea of millennials, then you must, by definition, reject the concept of proper segmentation and of consumers holding different perceptions and experiences."[7]

There's one brand that has not yet rejected such fundamentals. And that brand just happens to be the millennial marketer par excellence: Nike.

Focus on the global city dweller

In 2017 the shoe and sportswear company announced a new global strategy that was all about identifying segments and micro-targeting.

In this case, Nike aimed to develop what it called "local business, on a global scale" by concentrating all its attention upon the inhabitants of just 12 cities: London, New York, Los Angeles, Mexico City, Seoul, Beijing, Shanghai, Tokyo, Paris, Berlin, Barcelona and Milan.[8]

The objective was to get new products out faster to an elite group of world city customers and improve the levels of service they receive.

In being so focussed upon this niche, Nike hope to deliver 80% of the company's growth in the next two and half years.[9] Coupled with the recent announcement that it is pulling out of Amazon to better control brand, sales and customer relations, it's a bold strategy.[10] Especially when you're aiming to shift the 20 billion shoes you make a year. But, actually, it's not a new one.

Adidas had already decided to concentrate on a small number of "Key Cities" where they could get maximum impact from their marketing spend, catch the eye of the fashion conscious, global city-dweller and create trends that rippled outwards to the rest of the market.[11]

In comparison to the Heineken model of mass marketing to the millennials, this seems a lot smarter. Because it targets those with relatively more money, those who are open to new ideas, those who see their peer group as global rather than local, and those with influence on the street and in the media.

I said above that those who are peddling a purpose driven strategy do have a lucrative market. And this "Key City" audience – which encompassing everyone from millennials in Dalston and Peckham to the boomers in Islington and Chiswick – is it.

Who exactly are these folks?

Well, there's a clue in the work that Facebook did before the 2016 Presidential elections. Its data wonks segmented the US electorate by analysing, interests, religion, race, likes, dislikes, etc. And they discovered, much to Mark Ritson's delight, that: "There are millennials in Facebook's segmentation but, crucially, the data confirms that this is not one single homogenous group. Rather, there are three different types of millennial cohort when it comes to political activity and each has very different characteristics."[12]

Politically, they spread across the spectrum. There are those who form the conservative "Millennial Country

Culture" cohort. Those who sit amongst by far the largest grouping, the 40 million "Moderates". And then there are those who occupy the far left, the very liberal "Youthful Urbanites".[13]

It is the UK equivalent of these "Youthful Urbanites" who, I suggest, make up the main audience for our purpose-driven strategies. But, as I said above, they have older allies. Facebook's segmentation had these down as the "Politically Engaged City Dwellers".[14]

We'll get to meet them in a minute, but before then, let's look at the role purpose-driven brands play in their lives.

How brands work

We all know that purchase decisions are not only influenced by what the product does for us, how well it does it and what price point we can get it at.

The multi-billion-dollar business of branding is all about understanding, and presenting back to us, how that product makes us feel and what it says about us to the people who see us using it.

Take, for our purposes, the economic, cultural and social elite.

In the past, exclusive and expensive items – a Mulberry bag or a BMW perhaps – have been used by them as a means of advertising their superior status.

However, today such luxuries are commonplace.

Price wise, high end car marques have extended their ranges downwards, and generous leasing deals mean there are now half a dozen Beemers on every suburban street.

Meanwhile, most fashion houses have introduced entry-level accessories and, with the outsourcing of production to the Far East, their goods have flooded the markets and made them accessible to all but the poorest.

Actually, even the poorest can give their credit card a bashing if TK Maxx knocks down that pair of Miu Miu lace-up, metallic leather ballet flats from £388 a third and final time so you can now get them for just 35 quid.

So, with luxury being democratised in this way, how do the elites signify their status?

The new elite

Well, it is no longer through the expensive things they accumulate. Nor, indeed, is it necessarily their spending power.

Professor Elizabeth Currid-Halkett of the University of Southern California has called them "the Aspirational Class" and defined them as "partially an economic elite, but mainly a cultural elite. What we are observing with the 21st-century elite is a group that is defined by their cultural capital and the material goods that are essentially the physical embodiment of it."[15]

Currid-Halkett has borrowed from French polymath Pierre Bourdieu when she says that cultural taste is their way of differentiating themselves from – and signalling their superiority to – the rest of society. In his definitive work, *Distinction: A Social Critique of the Judgement of Taste*, Bourdieu said "Taste classifies, and it classifies the classifier."[16]

In truth, status seekers have been scoring points in this way for a long time. For example, the classical music snob might say she rates Alban Berg's atonal operas as far superior to the crowd-pleasers by Leoncavallo and Mascagni.

In classifying those two types of opera, the snob has thus classified herself – and enabled her to demonstrate her superiority over the oiks who love CavPag. Or, as she might have it, ChavPag.

Violent agreement

That's a dated example to be sure. For today, the things that matter are ideas, knowledge and what's trending intellectually. And it isn't opera, it's usually the op-ed in today's *Guardian*.

In "Thorstein Veblen's Theory of the Leisure Class – a Status Update", Rob Henderson explains: "The affluent have decoupled social status from goods, and attached it to beliefs ... instead of conspicuous consumption, you have conspicuous convictions."[17]

Currid-Halkett elaborates on this: "While their symbolic position sometimes manifests itself through material goods, mostly they reveal their class position through cultural signifiers that convey their acquisition of knowledge and value system – dinner party conversation around opinion pieces, bumper stickers that express political views and support for Greenpeace, and showing up at farmers' markets."[18]

If you've ever stopped at the farmers' market for your eco-friendly, vegan coffee (with Oatly Barista edition, of course) you'll know that the conversation often touches on one or other of the big social justice issues. If it doesn't, you'll have noticed that correct opinions on such matters are silently advertised on tote bags and T-shirts.

Either way, everyone will be in violent agreement, because this new aspirational elite "speak the same language, acquire similar bodies of knowledge and share the same values, all of which embody their collective consciousness."[19]

Meet the "Anywheres"

It's useful here to note that the clique identified by Professor Currid-Halkett fits snuggly into the social grouping that David Goodhart has described as the "Anywheres."

In his explanation of the gulf that divides UK society, *The Road to Somewhere,* Goodhart says that these predominantly London-dwellers make up only 20 per cent of the UK population and yet dominate our culture, society and industry.[20]

As with the Aspirational Class, they put a premium on education. Indeed, going to university is just another stopping off point in the peripatetic life they live. It's a journey that, in the course of their careers, will take them to the big city, be it here in the UK or elsewhere in the world.

These people are outward looking, happy with their metropolitan identities and see themselves as being from anywhere – hence Goodhart's designation.

They are undoubtedly the target for the HSBC poster that I saw recently.

> IF YOU WERE BORN IN ONE PLACE, GREW UP IN ANOTHER,
> BUT NOW LIVE SOMEWHERE COMPLETELY DIFFERENT
>
> ## WHERE ARE YOU FROM?
>
> TRICKY ONE. PERHAPS A BETTER QUESTION IS NOT
> WHERE ARE YOU FROM, BUT WHERE DO YOU FEEL AT HOME?

The implicit answer is, of course, anywhere.

Incidentally, you'll probably know that this is part of a campaign that aligns HSBC with the Anywheres – and by inference the Remain camp in the Brexit debate.

In so doing, the bank has chosen to antagonise the millions of customers and prospects who sit on the other side of an issue that has torn this country apart.[21] For example, in Leave-voting Blackpool, where I saw the poster, the above message would have gone down like a cup of sick.

We'll find out why later, but let's get back to the people who probably think HSBC's campaign is rather clever.

For them, globalisation has been a good thing. As is its concomitant, immigration. The woman who shares their hot desk at work is an enviably bright Brazilian, and the Deliveroo guy who brings their Avocado Mash for lunch is an amiable Romanian.

When it comes to their values, they mirror those of the left-leaning individuals who took Jonathan Haidt's test. According to Goodhart they are low on the three Binding ethics which Goodhart refers to as "identity, tradition and national social contracts." But they are high on Haidt's two Individualising values: human rights and social justice.[22]

Welcome to their neighbourhood

It must be stressed that while many of Currid-Halkett's Aspirational Class (and Goodhart's Anywheres) are moneyed, you don't need to be rich to join them.

Many of the younger ones are, for example, probably struggling to get on the property ladder. Meanwhile, their elders, whose dinner party conversation once revolved around how much the price of their property had risen since their guests arrived, might be trapped in negative equity.

But no matter, the Individualising values that inform their attitudes allow them to dwell in the most desirable of notional neighbourhoods.

It is a happy, secure place that epitomises all that a diverse community should be. Its residents are drawn from the broadest range of ethnic backgrounds and gender types. And, most importantly, to everyone's satisfaction, they can all be relied upon to hold exactly the same opinions.

It's the ideal location, in fact, for advertising and affirming one's elite status. For its elevated position gives you the perfect vantage point from which to look down upon the people below.

This neighbourhood is, of course, situated on that prime piece of real estate, the moral high ground.

When people in less salubrious neighbourhoods speak up – as with the Trump election and the Brexit vote – those on the moral high ground heighten the fortifications and lob abuse at those below.

They might borrow Hillary Clinton's description, "a basket of deplorables ... racist, sexist, homophobic, xenophobic, Islamophobic – you name it".[23] Or use Jo Swinson's put down from the Liberal Democrat Party's 2019 Conference, "insular, closed and selfish".[24]

They justify this aggressive disdain because, in their eyes, they are caring, open-minded and protective of the rights of others – and those they are attacking are not.

They are also better educated and work in the knowledge economy so, consciously or subconsciously, they regard themselves as intellectually superior.

As such, the decisions, actions and postures they adopt are informed by this sense of moral and intellectual superiority. They know better. Indeed, they ARE better.

Recognise anyone?

This feeling of innate superiority – and the need to display it – means that they are highly susceptible to advertising's social purpose strategies.

As Elizabeth Currid-Halkett pointed out in an interview with *Spiked* magazine: "There's a huge environmental and social consciousness that fits today's elite consumer. It's part of their cultural capital. So much of today's consumption is loaded with cultural capital."[25]

Whether it's organic fruit and veg in the fridge, fair trade tea and coffee on the shelf, slow fashion in the wardrobe or a couple of lines of "woke coke" in the bathroom, scored on the dark web direct from artisan farmers in Peru, there's a message in every purchase.

As such, our planners know they can push expensive items not on the strength of how good they are.

And not even on how much good they do.

But on how good they make the prospect feel when they buy them – and, crucially, when others see the prospect buying and using them.

If you're one of those planners then I'm sure you'll recognise plenty of your peers in the persona I've outlined above.

And hereby lies the danger. For many of us *are* the people described by Elizabeth Currid-Halkett. In her interview with *Spiked*, she described us to a T.

"We – the aspirational class – are in a bubble. And that bubble leaves out lots and lots of people. It's like when the liberal elite woke up the day after Trump's election victory, and were simply stunned at the result.

"I think it is important to notice that we are totally disconnected, and we need to find a way to connect."[26]

With specific reference to adland, it's a point made by Andrew Tenzer and Ian Murray: "The industry has lost touch with mainstream audiences . . . we need to develop a more pluralistic outlook."[27]

It's great advice but, as those chaps told us, our ethical

framework means it's highly unlikely we'll make that connection.

To see ourselves as others see us

The impact of blinkered self-righteousness on the people outside our bubble is put in its political context by lifelong Labour activist and trade unionist Paul Embery:

"You see, the group-thinkers and virtue-signallers and woke liberals and quasi-Marxists and echo-chamber-dwellers who comprise so much of the modern Left believe themselves to be Inherently Better People than those of us from the more traditional Left. We are Gillian Duffy and White Van Man of Rochester – ripe for votes, but not fit to be seen in public with."[28]

Again, I ask, do you recognise anyone here? Is this how our customers see adland?

And do we care either way? Well, on the evidence of the ads we're creating, not much.

Remember Jonathan Bottomley, the former Chief Strategy Officer at BBH and his view that: "We have lost the ability to make what we make interesting"?[29]

If that's true then isn't it because we've lost touch with what interests our audience in the first place?

Jonathan said we've replaced something that's meaningful to them with formulaic, repetitive messages and spam.

Andy Nairn, the much-respected planner and founder of Lucky Generals agrees. And, as far as he's concerned, it's all down to, yes, our lack of empathy for our audience. "I draw my conclusion from our collective output: ludicrous purpose-driven campaigns, clumsy attempts at personalisation, creepy retargeting and turgid content all point to an industry which is increasingly talking to itself." [30]

Making ads for ourselves

Orlando Wood, the author of *Lemon: How the Advertising Brain Turned Sour,* would tell you that Andy is describing work produced by a culture that's dominated by left brain thinking.

He'd also say that this left brain overreach explains adland's dearth of empathy.

Indeed, you can throw our lack of tolerance in there, too.

According to Orlando, "The self-referential nature of the left brain makes it difficult for it to see any other point of view, so group think, orthodoxy and dogma set in."

For good measure he adds: "It is goal oriented, seeking to manipulate and control the world through tools, through language and categorisation. It sees linear cause and effect, is self-conscious, literal, explicit and dogmatic, cutting off anything outside its model of the world." [31]

Our left brain thinking certainly explains the industry's embracing of identity politics and our moralising about social purpose.

And largely they are constructs of our own making. As Andrew Tenzer and Ian Murray point out in *The Empathy Delusion*, social purpose is "based on the assumptions and needs of the people in the advertising and marketing industry ... It is highly seductive to our industry on a personal level." [32]

This strongly implies that we are making ads for ourselves. And, if that's the case, what might be the long-term effects of this sanctimonious solipsism?

The diversity delusion

To be honest, ignoring the customer and making ads for ourselves is nothing new.

For example, 84% of the agency workforce is aged 18–40.[33] And doesn't it show in the work we produce? Can you remember anyone over the age of 40 appearing in a car commercial? Even though the average age of a new car buyer in the UK is 54.[34]

In an industry so committed to diversity, the above figure of 84% suggests that ageism doesn't rank high among the discriminatory practises that adland is trying so hard to stamp out.

Moreover, given that 88% of us have a degree or an MA, surely diversity also means having apprentice schemes for youngsters straight from school – and from schools outside the M25.[35]

And as for our working class representation. Well, Tenzer and Murray found that 70% grew up in a household where the chief income earner was social grade AB. This compares to just 29% of the modern mainstream.[36] As the typical adlander might say, "middle class, moi?"

But let's park the identity politics and return to my original point: will purpose-driven campaigns actually sell anything – and if not what will be the consequences?

Let's be positive and start with two that worked.

7
When purpose works – and when it doesn't

The US based retailer, REI, sells sporting goods, camping gear, travel equipment, and clothing. It also offers services such as outdoor-oriented vacations and courses.

The whole point of the business is to equip people to get into and enjoy the great outdoors.

Therefore it's understandable why the company gives financial support to conservation efforts, and sends volunteers to help with cleaning up, building new trails, and teaching children the importance of caring for the environment.

Such exemplary eco-friendly conduct should be grist for any good marketer's mill. Indeed, in 2016, REI's #OptOutside campaign was the worthy winner of nine Cannes Lions including the Titanium Grand Prix.[1]

Here's what happened: on Black Friday, retail's biggest day of the year, REI actually closed all its 150 stores. And, instead of buying its merchandise, potential customers were urged to avoid the mayhem of the malls and get out and about instead.

Many did. But not before going online and causing a 26% spike in online traffic to the REI site. The goodwill that this gesture generated could also be measured in the large number of new customers who then signed up to be members of the REI Cooperative.[2]

In short, not only did the promotion strengthen the bond between customer and REI but it also made the brand synonymous with getting out of the house, away from the crowds and back to nature.

Which must have been very good for future business.

It's good to talk

You'll find other examples of successful purpose-driven campaigns in such seminal works as Thomas Kolster's *Goodvertising* and Joey Reiman's *The Story of Purpose*.[3]

These books have inspired scores of businesses like Madlug, the Belfast-based social enterprise, that gives a backpack to a child in care for every one it sells. Or Brewgooder which donates the profit from every craft beer it sells to clean water charities.

These companies are making a difference right now, God bless 'em. However, for the most effective campaign with a social purpose as its business strategy, we have to go back 25 years.

According to the brief that BT gave its agency, the business problem it faced was "how do you persuade people (primarily men) to make more and longer telephone calls?" And the solution lay in "demonstrating the mutual benefits (emotional and rational) of making more calls."

The proposition that proceeded from there was "you can get more out of life and your relationships by communicating."[4]

Would anyone disagree? Surely not. And the way Abbott Mead Vickers communicated that promise turned social purpose into social engineering.

Take it from me, in those days men simply did not talk on the phone. If it rang, they'd wait until their wife picked it up. If she wasn't in, they'd ignore it or take a brief message for the missus and get her to call back later.

AMV pointed up both the absurdity of this behaviour and its social costs. And, with cockney tough guy Bob Hoskins as the spokesman, got millions of monosyllabic men to realise "It's Good to Talk".

As a result, BT made a lot of money from the campaign (an incremental £5 billion over the five years that it ran), rid itself of its "Britain's Most Hated Company" tag and really did change the world – in the UK at least.[5]

"Woke wash"

"It's Good to Talk" worked because the solution to the social problem came directly out of the functional role BT played in peoples' lives. Moreover, as with REI and environmental protection, the campaign strategy was congruent with BT's positioning.

As such, in both instances, the connection between social purpose and product benefit/brand idea was entirely credible.

But that's not the case with many of the brands who are new converts to this kind of thing.

The "woke wash", as Unilever's CEO, Allan Jope, called it is being walloped over those that have no connection with the cause they purport to support.[6]

They are, in fact, guilty of one of the most heinous crimes an advertiser can commit: borrowed interest. By that I mean, they try to grab the public's attention by saying something that has absolutely nothing to do with the benefit the product delivers.

Just think of Sunny Delight providing advice to the

suicidal. Ditto Axa Insurance. McDonald's offering succour to the bereaved. Cadbury Dairy Milk on loneliness among the elderly. M&S promoting LGBT rights with a lettuce, guacamole, bacon and tomato sandwich.

Or Heineken bringing peace to the culture wars.

Open your wallet

Mark Ritson watched the Heineken film – *Open Your World* – and felt it: "Might express all the right values, but marketers must remember if you don't use your budget to create sales, you've failed."

He continued: "Clearly the Heineken ad has created a dialogue and, hopefully, promoted a series of progressive causes and a whole notion of respect for divergent viewpoints. But what it will not do is help Heineken sell any more beer.

"What would have been the outcome had Heineken invested the money, time and other resources they ploughed into world peace and mutual understanding into selling a bit of beer with a strongly branded campaign for Heineken instead?"[7]

It's a good question. But the simple answer might be this: creating a strongly branded campaign for Heineken that sold a bit of beer is difficult. You need to write the brief, come up with a creative idea and execute it properly. And, in Heineken's case, you have to then make sure the finished film resonates in the dozens of markets in which you're competing.

We've already seen Gianluca di Tondo, Heineken's

Global Senior Brand Director, say why he made his ad. Using the common denominator of a social purpose made it easy for him to reach his millennial audience. "Millennials make my life easier" was his conclusion.[8]

I suppose Signor di Tondo should be commended for his candour. But while he stops short of calling the millennials suckers, you can't help think that he might be a little more discreet about his *modus operandi*. After all, if those suckers get wind of the purely pragmatic business reason why *Open Your World* was made, he could have a boycott on his hands.

That's a real danger for those brands who suddenly identify with discriminated against minorities and victims of prejudice. When waved by them, for example, the multi-striped Gay Pride banner often looks like a flag of convenience.

Sooner rather than later, the people they're targeting might realise that the brands are only adopting these causes because their focus groups and their data crunchers tell them to.

Moreover, if enough of these brands turn out to be hypocrites then the game really is up.

And worryingly, there's already no shortage of them.

Practise what you preach

Let's start with Starbucks. If you go to their site they'll tell you they are "known across the world as an ethical company" which has taken community-building as its mission.[9]

But as *The Guardian* reported in June 2019: "Starbucks UK-based European business paid just £18.3m in tax last year while paying the coffee giant's parent company in Seattle £348m in dividends collected for licensing the brand.

"In the UK, where there are about 1,000 Starbucks stores, the company paid just £4m of tax to the exchequer despite raking in £387m in sales."[10]

Not very community-minded, is it?

And remember Cadbury and its Dairy Milk campaign to get us all talking to our elderly neighbours? Well, in October 2019, *The Sun* ran this headline: "Fudge on Tax: Cadbury's US bosses paid just £271,000 in tax despite sales of £1.7billion in UK last year." Which means the company contributed bugger all to funding the care of the UK's ever-growing senior population.[11]

And how about the world's biggest brands: Apple, PayPal, Microsoft and Coca-Cola? When they criticised North Carolina's "Bathroom Law" as discriminatory against LGBT individuals, CNSNews.com pointed out their hypocrisy for doing big business in Middle Eastern countries where homosexuality and cross-dressing are punishable by fines, floggings, chemical castration, life imprisonment, or public execution.[12]

You'll find double standards on the agency side too. Do you remember the Cannes Lions delegate, Laura Jordan Bambach, telling *The Drum* how impressed she was with Extinction Rebellion? And how she thought we should get them in to our agencies and behind their fight against the climate emergency?

I'm sure she had a pile of briefs awaiting her return

from Cannes. One of which may well have been from her agency's biggest new busines win of the year, BetVictor. Yes, the largest independent bookmaker in the UK, and one of the merchants of human misery fuelling the country's gambling addiction epidemic.[13]

One wonders how the idealists at XR would feel about the ethics of that. Especially as BetVictor led the way when it came to tax evasion – taking the step in 1998 to move its entire business to Gibraltar in order to avoid HMRC.

The social cost of this was neatly explained on the forthright Mancunian blog *Nowt much to say*: "The double whammy with companies like BetVictor is that, as well as leaving the NHS to pick up the pieces when the fun stops – it's estimated that problem gamblers cost the government up to £1.2 billion per year – they are unwilling to pay the taxes to ensure that the NHS is adequately funded in the first place."[14]

Promoting such a business is mercenary, to be sure. But then again, you could make the argument that many purpose-driven strategies are, too.

After all, aren't they monetising and exacerbating psychological problems and social issues?

Exploiting weakness

Nick Asbury explained this in *Creative Review*: "They reinforce the insecurities they claim to fight and introduce new insecurities that people didn't know they were supposed to have. It's like that old joke about how to make someone feel insecure – tell them, I think you're great no matter what everyone else says."[15]

He goes on to make the equally valid point that, regardless of how complex and nuanced the social problem might be, brands come up with a platitudinous solution and cast themselves as the hero.

So, for example, at the conclusion of Heineken's *Open Your World* film, three issues that have split families and made mortal enemies out of lifelong friends are on their way to being resolved by a good chat over a bottle of beer. Heineken, naturally.

At least a solution is offered. No such panacea is provided in the multi-award winning *Viva la Vulva*. The blurb accompanying this film says, "More than half of women feel pressure for their genitalia to look a certain way."[16]

Do they? Really? Well such sub-navel gazing is perhaps a result of those First World, 21st century pastimes: spending too much time in online forums and watching too much pornography. But either way, I have news for those ladies.

A similar percentage of men worry about their genitalia. And have done for centuries. But hopefully our insecurities aren't going to be exploited by a film featuring singing bananas, baguettes, carrots, courgettes and, look away, chipolata sausages.

How to hide in a forest

But if we do get *Nob Gag: The Movie*, then we shouldn't be surprised. Clients are clients.

They're just doing what they are paid to do, and that is to make their numbers this quarter.

As I've said, they've embraced social purpose with much the same zeal as they did CRM, social media, behavioural economics and Big Data. And, in the same belief that, this time, they're onto a winner.

But are they right?

The *Havas Meaningful Brands 2019* report indicates that there is still a strong and growing preference for brands that take a stand on social and political issues.[17]

Which is probably why 2019 Pride was, as we've seen, supported by M&S's sandwich.

And Ikea, Dr Marten, Primark, Ralph Lauren, Boohoo, Adidas, the Co-op, Under Armour, Converse, Skittles, Virgin Atlantic, Reebok, Levi's, Apple, Banana Republic, Milk Makeup, Abercrombie & Fitch, Starbucks, Asos, Disney and Listerine.[18]

You can see the problem here can't you? As brands struggle to find a cause that hasn't already been adopted, how will they achieve that fundamental objective of smart brand management: differentiation? Shouldn't they remember that the best way to hide in an endangered forest is to dress as a tree?

Consumers certainly appear to be losing track of them.

Purpose fatigue?

The Havas research I referred to above suggests that consumers are "majorly underwhelmed by most brands". That's despite the deluge of issue-driven campaigns aimed at making that crucial emotional link between brand and prospect.

The conclusion seems to be that "these efforts are failing to make a connection either because they're lacking in authenticity or because consumers are fatigued by an overabundance of such campaigns."[19]

So what happens when two or three quarters pass and the numbers haven't been hit? Or when the CMO who launched the purpose-driven initiative moves on after their average 18 months in the hot seat is up?

Will their replacement stick steadfastly with the cause that their predecessor has hitched the company's bandwagon to? Or will they start looking elsewhere for, to use the words of the great Ad Contrarian, Bob Hoffmann, another of the "trendy fantasies that have dominated our industry for the past decade"?[20]

Signs are, it's already happening.

The next big thing

As we've seen, Accenture's 2018 report, *The Rise of the Purpose-Led Brand* gave marketers the evidence they needed to take a gamble on that strategy. Well, in 2019,

Accenture's analysts spread their chips onto another square.

On November 14th they released *AI: Built to Scale* and told us:

"84% of C-suite executives believe they must leverage artificial intelligence (AI) to achieve their growth objectives, yet 76% report they struggle with how to scale.

"Three out of four C-suite executives believe that if they don't scale artificial intelligence (AI) in the next five years, they risk going out of business entirely.

"Companies in our study that are strategically scaling AI report nearly 3X the return from AI investments compared to companies pursuing siloed proof of concepts."[21]

If this is where C-Level thinking is at, it is only a matter of time before their colleague from Marketing gets on board. And, of course, by then there'll be no shortage of advertising folk urging them along.

In fact, maybe it's only a matter of time before we see this article in the *FT*:

"P&G trimmed $100 million from its social purpose costs to see if anything happened. It didn't. Jon Moeller, the CFO explained: "We didn't see a reduction in growth rate (in value or volume of sales). What that tells me is that the spending we cut was largely ineffective."

I hope not. For the damage done to the advertising industry's reputation – and the brands whose purpose strategies we've been selling – will be cataclysmic.

8
Why we're losing touch with the people who matter most

The public already has little faith in us. As Gideon Spanier pointed out in *Campaign* magazine: "Public favourability towards advertising hit a record low of 25% in December 2018, according to [the think tank] Credos, which has previously found trust in advertising is 'in long-term decline'.

"Favourability has almost halved from 48% in 1992, the earliest point for which like-for-like data exists, but it has dropped even further from the 1960s, 1970s and 1980s".[1]

If we're seen to have used purpose as a marketing ploy, our "favourability" will fall through the floor. And those who bought into our messaging will be furious.

Damaging as that will be, we should be even more worried about those who, over the years, have had quite enough of being lectured to by the makers of everything from beer to burgers, tampons to trainers and supermarkets to whatever Sunny Delight purports to be.

I am talking about the most important group of all who, as everyone else seems to, we've thus far ignored.

At last, the Somewheres

We've touched upon them in reference to Jonathan Haidt's research. They're the ones with the fully formed value system that rests on both the Individualising and the Binding moral foundations.

They are also the counterpoint to David Goodhart's Anywheres. As he describes them, they are the 50% of the population who largely identify with the place where they were brought up. And they do so because, quite simply, they still live close to it. In fact, they are the three in five people in the UK who live within 20 miles of where they were at 14 years-of-age.[2]

They haven't moved out and adopted the persona of the metropolitan elite. They have roots. They have a sense of belonging. They are, as Goodhart says, from "Somewhere".[3]

It's their very parochialism that singles them out for opprobrium from the Anywheres. Indeed, they've been made to feel like strangers in their own country. As Ben Cobley's study of *The Tribe: The Liberal Left and the System of Diversity*, points out: "These people are not a part of this story, of the 'us', of 'our attitude', and 'our country'. According to the story, they have no part to play in the future, and have done nothing to build the present."[4]

When the cultural elites talk about them, it's with a mixture of condescension and contempt. (If you'd like a good example, see the BBC iPlayer commercials "Wasted on Some".)[5]

Not surprisingly, the Somewheres have had enough.

Indeed, when they think they're being talked down to, you might call them "the angry mainstream." And, we should watch out, because they often get that feeling when they're on the receiving end of the latest social purpose campaign.

Mind the gap

As Andrew Tenzer and Ian Murray tell us: "Using virtue to stand out is of little value if all it means is projecting our values onto others."[6]

When advertising does this it is, as David Goodhart says, another example of "imposing Anywhere priorities on Somewheres who have different ones."[7]

And the effect of that is twofold.

It confirms the suspicion that the liberal left no longer shares the economic/social interests of the people for whom it used to speak. It has a new agenda.

And, in constantly pushing this agenda, it provides cultural conservatives with just more evidence that their mores, values and traditions are under attack from the corporate, intellectual and cultural institutions that run their lives.

Indeed, the liberal left's fixation on race, the environment, gender and diversity isn't bringing people together, it is pushing us apart.

Orlando Wood, whose expertise lies in measuring and tracking the effectiveness of advertising, explains that: "Disruptive purpose advertising tends to pitch one set of moral values against another [which] stokes and perpetuates divisions. Advertisers use shock tactics in the hope of galvanising the populace, but in so doing they run the risk of talking down to it. This will not promote trust in advertising among the public any more than in the brands it represents."[8]

Tenzer and Murray concur: "Marketing strategies

driven by narrow foundations only serve to widen the cultural gap between brands and the very people they are seeking to engage."[9]

Netflix versus soap operas

Not that the Somewheres are opposed to social justice. As we've noted, their behaviour is also informed by Haidt's Individualising ethics. But their closer communitarian ties mean that looking out for the underdog is more likely to be seen in caring for a neighbour than campaigning for Syrian refugees.

You could say that if the liberal likes people in general, the conservative likes them in particular.

Socially the former are likely to be found in front of their screens watching the next big thing on Netflix – and then storing up cultural capital by talking about it on social media. Conversely, the Somewheres go out and play an active part in an ongoing soap opera where they, their friends and neighbours each have a well-defined role and identity.

Given this strong attachment to local relationships, community, place and belonging, Somewheres are likely to protect their shared values from too rapid a pace of change. While those values continue to work for them, they're in no rush to swap them for others being imposed from beyond.

Joan C. Williams saw this response in her analysis of America's white working class and observed: "For many perfectly able working class people, their dream is not to join the upper middle class with its different culture but to stay true to their own values in their own communities, just with more money."[10]

Pushing back

The extent to which America's working classes and, indeed, the mainstream are pushing back was revealed by in depth research that was conducted by the More in Common Community, which was founded in memory of Jo Cox, the MP murdered by a right-wing fanatic in the run-up to the Brexit referendum.

While looking at such issues as immigration, the extent of white privilege, and the prevalence of sexual harassment, the authors described 8% of Americans as "progressive activists". In contrast, the report found that two-thirds of Americans make up what it termed the "exhausted majority." Their members "share a sense of fatigue with our polarized national conversation, a willingness to be flexible in their political viewpoints, and a lack of voice in the national conversation."[11]

Christine Wise, Chief Strategy Officer at Seattle-based agency, DNA, found much the same thing from her research. And in her November 2019 *Campaign* article, "Consumers want brands to heal divisions", she explained:"For the vast majority of people, their concerns are less focused on politics and societal issues and more focused on the personal worries and struggles of daily life.Across all generations, the two top personal priorities heading into 2020 are improving their physical health and personal finances. In fact, what the majority of people want from brands today is for them to help build common ground, avoid taking sides, and support their personal priorities."[12]

What they don't want are lessons in political correctness. Going back to the More in Common research, of the general population 80% believe "it is a problem in our country." This includes 74% aged 24 to 29, and 79% under age 24. Which indicates that, when it comes to being PC, the woke are in a clear minority across *all* ages.[13]

People here in the UK are also tired of being told what to think, say and do.

In August 2019, Sophia Gaston, Visiting Research Fellow at the LSE explained that: "A new survey I have conducted with pollsters Opinium finds that railing against political correctness is so ingrained in the British character, it could be described as a national pastime. Three-quarters of Britons believe that political correctness goes too far and exceeds common sense."[14]

Meet France's angry Somewheres

Such social/cultural conservatism should be respected, and not derided or misinterpreted as the behaviour of a bunch of know-nothing reactionaries.

But do we in adland respect and empathise? I think we know the answer to that.

To borrow Paul Jankowski comment on the situation in the US, our "continued personal biases can affect an entire campaign's message, based on a lack of qualitative understanding of what makes the population segment tick. An innate, negative point of view has the effect of boxing out real insights."[15]

And pissing people off.

We've seen in France what happens when they get really angry.

Over there, they too have their Somewheres. In his *Twilight of the Elites*, Social Geographer Christophe Guilluy identifies them as the "Peripherals".[16] These people live in France's small to medium sized towns and feel starved of the economic opportunities, social mobility and cultural stimulation that are monopolised by the globalised hubs, Paris, Lyon and Bordeaux.

It is they who have led the *gilets jaunes'* violent rebellion against the patronising power elites.

Guilluy has identified that clique as the urban, hipster *bourgeois-bohemes* or *bobos* – most of whom would be as at home in Soho as they are in SoPi.

Our own *bourgeois-bohemes* who dominate our media aren't quite as hated, but we're getting there. And the danger lies in us making stands that drive us further away from the mainstream.

Which side of history are you on?

The gap widened again when, on October 21st, 2019, Tim Lindsay, the CEO of D&AD took to Twitter to promote the D&AD Impact Awards. These are given "to anyone using creative thinking as a catalyst for positive change". In short, those promoting the progressive left's favourite causes: diversity, equality, sustainability etc.

Just in case anyone failed to get onboard with the awards – and the agenda they promote, Tim's tweet issued this warning: "As individuals, companies and an industry we are going to be forced to make decisions about which side of history we want to be on in the climate emergency. And those choices are going to have to be made uncomfortably soon."[17]

Now Tim's commitment to this cause is unwavering and sincere. But there may be hints here of what Orlando Wood sees as left brain thinking. In *Lemon*, Wood says an "eyes of history are upon us", truth or lies approach typifies the left brain's mode of attending to the world. It tends to be "controlling and dogmatic", leaning toward "simplified" choices and away from the idea that two opposing views (in this case, for example, arguments around green colonialism) can co-exist – with the truth lying somewhere in between.[18]

It is also remarkable for its presumption. A point that, in this case, would not be lost on the people outside advertising's bubble.

The Trinity Mirror's Reach Research team assessed advertising's significance in the lives of these people in its White Paper, "When Trust Falls Down". It concluded that "advertising is no longer considered to be a central part of popular culture – shaping the conversation in the way it has in the past ... people outside London are significantly more likely to hold this opinion (50%) than those living in London (35%).

"The uncomfortable truth is that people are nowhere

near as informed about advertising as the industry thinks. This only reinforces the argument that brands and the advertising industry are often marketing inside their own echo-chamber."[19]

To those people, Tim taking the offensive in the modern culture wars would be seen as just another example of overreach by the metropolitan elites.

Actually, they'd think nothing of the sort. Friends in my home town would say: "He's got a bloody brass neck".

An unwise, binary choice

The "which side of history are you on?" challenge is dangerous for three other reasons.

First, for most people, the climate emergency is not a priority. It might be for Tim and those who share his extreme concern. But they are in the minority.

Indeed, when environmental campaigners have been given the opportunity to put their argument to the public, this is what has happened: At the 2015 general election, the Green Party crashed through the one million vote barrier to take 1,111,603.

Since then, the climate emergency has never been out of the headlines. If that coverage had been generated by a global advertising campaign, the media cost would have been in the billions. Yet, in the recent general election, the Green Party's vote dropped to 850,000.[20]

To the electorate, the environment was not even of secondary importance. Which leads me to think it would be unwise for the advertising industry to force a binary choice. For it would put us at odds with – and, by implication, morally condemn – the millions of people we and our clients seek to engage on a daily basis.

"Advertising suffers when it preaches"

Having said that, most people we're selling to get the message about the need to look after the planet. They feel that in their own ways, they are doing their bit. However, they could be persuaded to do a lot more by messages that are more, yes again, empathetic – and which connect with the Binding ethical values that inform their lives.

But, as the research I've cited above indicates, they don't enjoy being talked down to, and they're likely to resist Tim's portentous moralising – and any advertising that reflects it.

In a *Marketing Dive* article titled, "How tone-deaf activism risks eroding brands", John Matejczyk, the Co-Founder and Chief Creative Officer of M/HVCCP offered this considered view: "As with any art, advertising suffers when it preaches".[21]

And finally, well, I'll bow to the wisest man in advertising, Jeremy Bullmore: "Advertising's role is to provide best advice to clients on how to meet their business objectives. And then to harness what skills it has in order to achieve those objectives. It has no remit to take stands or choose sides on political, cultural or social issues. And the moment it does so, its judgement is compromised."[22]

For the many not the few

Although the clique we belong to – Currid-Halkett's Aspirational Class – consider ourselves to be classifiers of taste, as advertising men and women we cannot be its arbiters.

We are not presenting our audience with a pair of French windows and then inviting them to step through into what we've shown them is a better world.

We are holding up a mirror to theirs. And if what they see doesn't reflect their reality, they'll ignore or reject it.

When it comes to pushing the progressive ideas that are so dear to our industry's heart, we should remember that we're producing work for the many, not the few. And that the UK is a small 'c' conservative country.

The recent general election result proved that. The most radical left-wing Labour manifesto ever presented to the public resulted in that party's worst defeat since 1935.

You might explain Labour's defeat upon the Brexit issue. But then you have to realise that Brexit appeals to those who are united by a sense of place, belonging and rootedness – i.e. the conservative values that Jonathan Haidt described as "Binding".

To put it mildly, these communitarian, patriotic Somewheres did not share the Anywheres' enthusiasm for the EU's cosmopolitanism.

"There is a clear message to our industry"

If you still don't buy the idea that this country is intrinsically conservative, consider this: if the Tories win the next general election, the Labour Party will have been in power for just 13 of the past 50 years.

And remember, those victories were won by the moderate, centrist party of New Labour. In its early years at least, its strategists were fixated on keeping in step with the electorate. Whilst sometimes derided as "death by focus group", this attention to the popular mood was a key to its success.[23]

It's a habit that the ad folk promoting social purpose strategies would do well to develop. Otherwise they'll drift further apart from an increasingly hostile audience.

Indeed, according to Xavier Rees, the CEO of Havas London and Havas helia, the general election result indicated that we need to rethink our entire relationship with the public.

"Regardless of your political allegiances, there is a clear message to our industry. The London mindset is not shared by the rest of the country and the echo chamber that we inhabit does not reflect the views and experiences of the nation as a whole. We would do well to heed it as we seek to make our work resonate more strongly with the British people."[24]

Put another way, we talk a lot about the importance of engagement and storytelling. But the reality is that people will only engage with what we're saying when they can see themselves in the stories we are telling.

And to achieve this, we must set those stories in the

world in which they live. And not the world as we see it –
or want it to be.

Adland's first bare bum ...

Here are a couple of examples of how even the best
amongst us can get it wrong.

Back in early 2001 when my agency was sharing a
building with RKCR/Y&R, their brilliant planner, MT
Rainey, told me about the new commercial for Marks &
Spencer and how it would transform the brand's image.

It featured a size 16 women running up a hill and
shedding her clothes en route until she stood bare-ass
naked on top shouting "I'm normal!".

This celebration of the less than conventionally perfect
body shape came several years before Dove took the
same line with its Campaign for Real Beauty.

As Dove's more modest expression of femvertising was
gradually gaining traction, the M&S film was being
described in *The Guardian* as "disastrously unpopular"
and blamed for putting the business "on the brink of
disaster."[25]

Clearly it was too much, too soon for the middle
Englanders who were M&S's market. So, in light of this
conservative response, the agency set about repairing the
damage by reverting to M&S's core historical attributes of
quality, service and value.

And, in the hugely successful campaign that followed,
who did they get to represent those values? Homely,
lovely – and still rather skinny – Twiggy.[26]

... and gay kiss

I started this essay with reference to my friend Patrick Collister. When first we met, 25 years ago, he had one of the biggest jobs in the industry: Executive Creative Director at Ogilvy and Mather Advertising.

One day we were having a drink and he told me he was very excited about the new Guinness commercial he was working on. It was, he said, the best thing he'd done in the four years he'd been in that top job.

He explained what happened in the film and how it ended with the startling revelation that the domestic partners at the centre of the story were men. And how the spot concluded with the first gay kiss in advertising history.

"Wow", said I, "do you think you'll get it past the client?"

He smiled triumphantly and said, "Tony Kaye's shot it. It's already done, and they've bought it!"

And at which we both got drunk.

Two weeks later, when we next met, he told me the sobering truth that news of the ad had got out, the response hadn't been great and the client had not only pulled it, they'd even denied it existed.

They realised the public weren't ready for Patrick's first gay kiss.

I was. He was. Everyone we'd spoken to was up for it. But those outside our bubble were not.

And the probable reaction of the man in the street became apparent when *The Sun* stuck a pink pint of Guinness on the newspaper's front page above the headline, "Bottoms Up."[27]

Keeping pace, not setting it

Today, mainstream values have changed and, for example, we're all used to seeing *Coronation Street's* gay priest, Billy, sucking the face off his various boyfriends.

But we're still waiting for advertising's first gay peck on the cheek. Which indicates that, far from leading the way, we have to stay a couple of steps off the pace of social and cultural developments.

If we cannot exercise this self-restraint when working for our commercial clients, then we should follow the example of a great hero of mine, Howard Gossage.

It was he who said "Changing the world is the only fit work for a grown man," and he tried to do so in several ways.

For one, he always treated his audience with admirable respect, and introduced a form of interactive advertising that allowed them to enter into a dialogue with him. It was highly effective.

He was also the first adman to incorporate media into his communication strategy. The ad, or in many cases the promotional stunt, was there to stimulate further coverage in newspapers, radio, TV and any other medium Gossage could harness.

When he became disillusioned with applying his talents to the benefit of commercial clients, he put both these techniques to the service of not-for-profit organisations. Most famously, in 1966 he helped the Sierra Club to stop the damming of the Grand Canyon and kickstarted both the Green Movement and Friends of the Earth.[28]

Until his death in 1969, he never again worked for his commercial clients.

In so doing, he followed the golden rule laid down by his great contemporary, Bill Bernbach: "A principle isn't a principle until it costs you money".[29]

And that, in conclusion, is what we who work in advertising today should consider.

Ask your clients what they hire you for

Until the system changes, the rope still binds us to the capitalists who make that system work.

If you're in any doubt, ask your clients what they hire you for. It might be a husband and wife who have mortgaged their home and sold their car in order to do their start-up. Or it could be the CEO of a multinational which directly and indirectly provides employment and income to hundreds of thousands of people.

All three depend on your mastery of competitive persuasion to help them sell their products and services.

Or, to return to my original analogy, they rely on the rope that ties you and them together i.e. the shared interest in making their capitalist endeavour work.

If this goes against your principles then do as Gossage did and detach the rope.

But if you are not willing to cut yourself free, and if you're happy to exchange your talents for their money then you should perhaps consider this last piece of advice from Mr Bernbach:

"The purpose of advertising is to sell. That is what the

client is paying for and if that goal does not permeate every idea you get, every word you write, every picture you take, you are a phony and you ought to get out of the business."[30]

9
So what would I do if I was you?

Still with me? Good. Thank you.

I thought I might lose one or two of you at page 27. Or maybe page 55. Or perhaps page 79.

I've already been dropped by a couple of left-leaning industry friends who I've known for years. I'd asked them to read my manuscript, and I suppose they just wanted to prove my point about the low tolerance threshold of people of their political persuasion.

In anticipation of further hostility, I toyed with calling this chapter: "The longest suicide note in history".

However it was always my aim to provoke a debate and challenge the industry's groupthink. What's more, as a direct marketer, generating a response is my schtick, so if you'd like to get in touch, I'm here: harrisosteve@googlemail.com

But before that, please bear with me. I realise I've been critical of how a left-leaning industry has parted ways with its audience and given up on value propositions in favour of progressive causes.

So I think I owe you an explanation as to how I might negotiate the woke-infested waters that agency chiefs have to get through today.

Advertising's existential crisis

In her analysis of a turbulent past 12 months in adland, *Campaign's* Claire Beale spoke about the existential crisis that has left agencies desperately searching for their purpose.

As Claire says, an agency faces two major dilemmas. Does it choose or reject its clients on the basis of that client's record on the salient social justice issues of the day?

And, how does the industry attract and keep young and talented people who need a good reason to turn up for work each morning.[1]

Well things have changed a lot since I ran my agency, but here's what I'd do.

First, I'd try to avoid the sanctimony and hypocrisy that flourish in the absence of a clear definition of best practise.

Carol Cone, CEO of Carol Cone ON PURPOSE, pointed out the problem when she said: "Browse the websites of purpose agencies and you'll find more definitions of purpose than you can count on one hand. (We conducted a recent analysis and found 20 in just an hour of research.)"[2]

Given this lack of clarity, purpose is being used selectively by those who say one thing and do another.

So, if I was running a shop now and I was aiming to say one thing and actually *do* it, I would try to gain B-Corp accreditation.[3]

To achieve this, I'd have to see if the principles that guided me and my partners, Tim Patten and Martin Troughton, have stood the test of time.

What about an agency's "purpose"?

Let's start by answering Claire Beale's question about our "purpose".

That was simple: to run an agency that produced happy and productive people.

We figured that's your fundamental responsibility as a manager. If the people you work with are miserable, it's your fault. And your business will be in trouble.

Which is why we tried to make life in the agency as interesting as possible. To achieve that we set our stall at making that rare thing: a quality product that everyone could be proud of.

Craftsmanship over mass production. Involvement over alienation. Excitement over drudgery.

We tried to give our people a sense that what they did mattered. And that it was essential that they cared about doing it well.

When I was reading the touching speech that David Droga made after being awarded The Lion of St Mark at Cannes in June 2017, I recognised a bit of what we were trying to do:

"I would put down everything in my career to the fact that I cared – about what I do, who I work with, what I make. Caring makes you want to work harder. People can't pay you to care. People can't teach you to care. But when you find something you care about, you give it everything. You never settle. You are always pushing to learn and be better and support those around you. All I've tried to do in my career is care. That's all we need to do. More agencies need to give a shit, work hard and try to make beautiful and impactful things."[4]

Wonderful, inspiring stuff. And I'd agree with all of the above. But I'd add that if caring can't be taught then it can be encouraged. Indeed, we accepted that it was our responsibility to create an environment in which our people *could* care.

And it was this that dictated which clients we worked with.

How to choose your clients

It goes without saying that we'd have nothing to do with tobacco or gambling. Nor were we interested in selling crap products like fast foods, fizzy drinks and other junk.

To get the business we wanted, the decision process was actually pretty simple. We would ask ourselves three questions – two of which had to be answered "yes".

[ ] Will we be able to do creative we'll all be proud of?

[ ] Will we make money from the relationship?

[ ] Will we all enjoy working with this client?

Question 1's box always had to be ticked. Otherwise we would say "no" from the off.

If Question 2 was a "yes" then all well and good.

But if not and we thought we'd enjoy the experience then we ticked box 3.

Enjoying it was as important as making money. Sometimes more so.

In Virgin Atlantic and Granada Sky Broadcasting, we had two lucrative clients for whom we were doing good work.

They were, however, rude to our people and showed them little respect. So, we had no choice but to let them go.

Even more costly was our decision not to work with Ford. When Martin Troughton and I took control of Wunderman, the Ford account was a separate entity within the group. We were often asked by the network to take them on. Which was tempting because Martin and I were on a five year earn out and the addition of Ford's huge revenues to our bottom line would have trebled our final pay off.

But the massive workload that came with Ford would have snuffed out the agency's creative spark and made us all miserable. So we turned it down.

Of course, as part of a network, sometimes you have to take delivery when the lorry load of fresh compromises arrives at your door. And we were forced by the bosses in New York to work on Microsoft on their terms not ours. Which meant it was very hard to answer questions 1) or 3).

So we put this giant piece of business in quarantine in the hope it didn't infect the rest of the agency, while we battled to win the client over. Unfortunately, for those who worked on it, we never really did.

What Gossage taught us about fighting causes

We already had enough big corporate clients. And doing good creative for them was always a challenge. So we tried to sugar the pill by asking our staff to bring in businesses they'd like to work on.

This had the double advantage of also allowing the agency to work with very small outfits and start-ups who needed a leg up. Some were high street shops. Others were manufacturers with little more than a big idea to be going along with.

For example, I remember Polly Jones bringing in a drink company called Innocent. Alas, they didn't buy any of the ideas we came up with. I wonder what happened to them.

Such projects allowed our staff to have a bit of fun whilst also supporting businesses, charities and causes they liked.

If we ran the agency today, I'm sure colleagues would bring in their favourite purpose-oriented causes, and we'd be happy to put our voluntary efforts behind them. But, in so doing I'd remind everybody of Howard Gossage's approach. He, the greatest of advertising's cause-related campaigners, felt most agencies made the mistake of talking *at* their audience.

"Carrying on a monologue in this way alerted them [the audience] to the problem without giving them any means of doing something about it. So rather than embracing the cause, these potential advocates turned against it out of guilt for their own inactivity. As Gossage explained 'what you've got to do is give people recourse. You've got to give them something to do so they don't feel guilty and therefore hate you for making them feel guilty'".[5]

In short, instead of the scaremongering and hectoring that characterise much of the work we see today, I'd recommend Gossage's empathetic, interactive approach.

Having said that, I imagine we'd be doing little other overtly purpose-driven work.

Why we wouldn't be purpose-driven

The answer brings us back to selling.

To this end, the main thing we drummed into our people was the notion that all effective advertising is an exercise in Problem/Solution.

At the start of every brief, we asked two questions that ensured that the prospect's needs were at the core of our communications.

1. What is the problem facing my prospect at the moment?
2. What is the solution provided by the product/ service or brand that I am selling?

If we couldn't answer those questions, we told our clients not to waste their money advertising.

The solution always came from the practical or psychological benefit delivered by the thing we were selling. It was expressed as a single-minded proposition – and that is what the creative work would be about.

I'm afraid to say, that if I was operating today very few purpose-driven proposition would get my sign off. Which means we'd do very little "socially meaningful" work. (And win very few Cannes Lions as a result).

If you think I need to apologise for this, may I cite Simon White, the Chief Strategy Officer of FCB West, as my witness for the defence.

"While people care about social issues, it's not why they're buying the brand. Most of the time people choose whichever brand best meets their goals. These are both functional goals, and unconscious emotional goals linked to our deeper human drives.

"When brands advertise their favorite social cause, instead of meeting consumers' goals, the advertising becomes irrelevant, ineffective and annoying."[6]

In effect, the agency is doing ads for itself. Or perhaps for a like-minded client who they know will buy the strategy.

But they are ignoring the target audience's most pressing need. And, as a result, the work won't sell.

How to attract and train the talent you need

If today that would deter people with a heightened woke sensibility from joining us, then all the better.

Indeed, I believe the answer to Claire Beale's question about hiring the best lies in aiming for *cognitive* diversity. Which means recruiting from outside the bubble in which the industry is trapped and attracting people who will challenge our groupthink mentality.

One of our best teams were a couple of talented young lads, Alan Wilson and Diccon Driver. They'd come down from Liverpool and Stevenage, and were sleeping on a friend's floor when we gave them a start.

I don't know whether they had degrees. And it didn't matter. For, while we didn't go so far as to seek out Dominic Cummings's "weirdos and misfits", our aim was to recruit curious people (in both senses of the word).[7] And preferably those with some experience of real life.

Then we set about teaching them the necessary skills.

At least once a fortnight there'd be a compulsory session on writing a brief ... trafficking work ... having an idea ... coming up with a headline ... writing copy ... selling the creative ... running a meeting ... organising a pitch ... that kind of thing.

Then they got their training on the job – where everyone shared the grunt work and everyone had a crack at the sexy stuff.

An Account Exec met clients, wrote briefs, and sold work. There were no rigid job demarcations. In the creative department, the only title anyone really wanted was Award-Winning Copywriter or Award-Winning Art Director.

If that Art Director or Account Exec felt they needed some external training, or they wanted us to get a speaker in from outside, they had only to ask. If they preferred to invite their clients along, all the better.

As I said, we spent a lot of time training our people to do work that sold. And to achieve that we encouraged them to not only study and practise their craft but to also take an interest in life beyond advertising.

If there was a book, a magazine or a comic they wanted, we paid for it. Moreover, we covered their admission to the theatre, the pictures, art galleries and exhibitions.

Nowadays that's quite common but 20 years ago it was unusual.

Likewise our decision to pay them double if they took a two-week holiday rather than a one-week break. We wanted them to go further, stay away longer, forget work, get a fresh perspective and come back with new ideas.

And not just ideas that could be used in our strategies, creative and production, but also about how the agency should be run.

Giving your people their say

To invite their feedback, we had a question box open in the agency into which colleagues could anonymously post their comments – and their criticism.

Then, every three months, Martin and I would empty the box on a table and, in front of the entire agency, read them out. None were edited. And, no matter how hostile, we tried to answer them.

As I've said, our aim was to produce happy and productive people. And if that meant clearing the air (and getting a bit of a kicking) on a regular basis, that was fine by us.

And I think we got some of the way there.

Of course, there'll be former colleagues reading this who were distinctly *unhappy* during their (usually) brief time at our agency. I make no apology for sorting wheat from chaff. Indeed, I was obliged to do so out of respect for those who were working hard and delivering.

Indeed, we often got rid of people only after their peers had berated Martin and I for making the mistake of hiring them in the first place. As we used to say, the white corpuscles will reject the virus. And the body will return to health.

A force for good? You tell me

Would this approach, this raison d'etre, this purpose pass muster today? Where, you might be justified in asking, is the commitment to bigger causes?

Well, I always felt that creating 160 jobs from absolutely nothing was quite a big thing for Martin and I to do.

Producing work that sold things and therefore kept many thousands of people employed at Xerox, Microsoft, IBM, Vodafone, Rolls-Royce Motor Cars, Jaguar, M&G Investments, San Miguel, Samsung, etc was, in its own way, beneficial to our fellow men and women. So, too, was the money and awareness we raised for the likes of Macmillan Cancer Support, Anxiety UK and the Royal Marsden Hospital – often for no fee.

If that seems pretty circumspect in today's idealistic climate, then I must admit, our aim was never to change *the* world. But, in focusing on producing happy and productive people, our aim was to change *their* world.

To give them a place they enjoyed coming to; a sense of pride in their achievements; and the skills to master their craft and command the respect of their peers.

On the latter point, I hope they also enjoyed the satisfaction of knowing that, in their discipline, they'd helped build the best creative shop in the world.

Finally, we taught them how to sell things. Which, in an industry that's largely given up on that, will have kept them in gainful and, hopefully, happy employment since their time with us.

And perhaps, in its own small way, that has been a force for good.

10
Commercial purpose or social purpose? Adland's response to Covid-19 and the post-pandemic recession

And, with that upbeat and slightly self-congratulatory flourish I thought I'd ended the book.

That was on March 1st.

On the following day, I sent the manuscript to the publisher, convinced it carried a vital message that the advertising industry urgently needed to hear.

The book came back on March 20th. By then adland was, like everyone else, preoccupied by the rather more urgent need to survive Covid-19.

The things I wanted to draw the industry's attention to would have to wait.

So I settled for a soft launch in April and set about writing an additional chapter that took on board the impact of Covid-19 and the advertising and marketing community's response to it during the first three months of the crisis.

I was encouraged to do this by Paul Burke who, early on, told me that my focus on the importance of selling things would be infinitely more relevant once the post-pandemic recession hit.

Clients who had been starved of custom and who had just enough capital to see them through the next few months would need the cash registers to ring as never before.

And agencies, who'd been playing fast and loose with the confidence of C-suite executives would be forced to dramatically prove their worth by generating the sales that would keep their clients trading.

In fact, for all concerned, it would be a case of We Sell – Or Else We Go To The Wall.

April is the cruellest month

As The Wall's stygian shadow lengthened over adland, Craig Mawdsley, Joint Chief Strategy Officer at Abbott Mead Vickers/BBDO spoke of "the biggest global event since the Second World War."[1]

He wasn't kidding. On April 14th, the IMF predicted that the "Great Lockdown Recession" would be the steepest in almost a century. Global Gross Domestic Product would shrink by 3% – dwarfing the 0.1% contraction of the 2009 financial crisis.[2]

Petrified, nine out of ten marketers delayed their campaigns, new business evaporated and Mark Ritson warned that advertising investment would be reduced by 30-60% over the rest of 2020 and beyond.[3]

WPP reported a 7.9% slump in net sales for March and, within days, the holding company's CEO, Mark Read, was announcing "an undisclosed number of permanent headcount reductions."[4]

Across the industry, many of those who weren't fired were furloughed. Which meant, for most of them, going to The Wall had been delayed rather than averted.

By the end of April, *Campaign* announced that its readers had accepted there'd be no UK ad market recovery before 2021.[5]

The magazine's Gideon Spanier reported there would be a 39% drop in the three months to June, Q3 would be down 24% and Q4 down 9%. "The numbers point to a 16.7% or £4.2 billion slump for the year – worse than the 2008-2009 financial crisis ... It is impossible to believe there will be a rapid recovery to full economic health."

The scale of the advertising downturn was, he said, "appalling".[6]

Pivoting at the speed of culture

It was, to use the crisis's most commonly used adjective: unprecedented. And, given there was no App to plot a way through the uncertainty, the industry's leaders seemed lost.

Most spoke about "the new normal". A lot were "pivoting" (there's one coming up in a minute). And the trendiest were "moving at the speed of culture" which, in the old normal, was called "being topical".

On April 20th, *Campaign's* Claire Beale spelt it out or, to be precise, punctuated it out when she wrote: "Everything. Has. Changed."[7]

Three days later, her magazine asked what skills would be most in demand as the post-pandemic recession bit.

Suffice to say, no one mentioned a talent for competitive persuasion or the ability to sell things.

Sally Quick, Partner, Mission Bay was sure that "More than ever, the ad industry is going to need open and empathetic trust builders, who can tap into the zeitgeist, 'read the room' and display their passion and purpose."[8]

Just a minute

Harjot Singh, Chief Strategy Officer Europe and UK, McCann Worldgroup took a deep breath and off he went: "The industry will recover using this crisis as a pivot towards even greater ambition and creativity lead (sic) by self-aware, emotionally intelligent and decisive leaders." Warming to his theme he continued: "Exceptionally creative and strategic problem-solvers who demonstrate high levels of adaptive intelligence will be most in demand. Adaptive intelligence will be most sought after because it's a skill that hinges on an attitude of creativity, resilience and EQ, as much as it does on proven technical prowess of rapid innovation, applying and envisioning data/technology in the most creatively and commercially effective ways, and seamless stakeholder management."

At which Nicholas Parsons gave him one point for speaking for 60 seconds without repetition, deviation or hesitation. But deducted two points because no one could understand a blessed thing he'd said.[9]

Helen Kimber, Managing Director of the headhunting firm, The Longhouse, gave us the advertising equivalent of speaking in tongues: "Technical skills and personal qualities. Leaders with conviction, confidence, but crucially empathy too – not only for people but clients needing to completely reinvent their businesses. Leadership breeding partnership and supportive solutions. Set direction, but seek advice, flex and adapt in our approach to projects, fees, process and delivery. A tightrope between conviction and flexibility. Brands need us to re-establish lighthouse statuses, simultaneously connecting on an intimate and authentic level.

"Bigger strategic thinking; consultancy approach, willingness to be generous with creativity without the same production payoff. Creatively, polymaths who glide effortlessly across the communication landscape, applauding pragmatic, practical creatives who can learn new technical skills and deliver with limited resources. In delivery, resurgence of the multitasker and integrated CV. Less bodies, more inventive solutions across channels. Those with a zig-zag of experience will be in high demand. Similarly, the ambidextrousness of combined client service/project management; ability to manage *and* make."[10]

As I said, adland's leaders were lost but, alas, not for words.

Fighting talk

Cometh the hour, cometh . . .

. . . David Sable, the former Global CEO of Y&R, who we last met on page 25 heading off to Hoboken in search of some real consumers.

When all around him were floundering, he reassured us that "Leadership is about leaders. It's a big word that doesn't mean much because we don't have any leadership without leaders."[11]

Hmm.

Thankfully, in stepped *Campaign's* Gideon Spanier who, incidentally, has managed to talk sense throughout this crisis: "Advertising and media leaders should be fighting loudly for the importance of investing in brands as adspend has collapsed . . . The ad industry needs to get ready. We need more case studies that prove the value of advertising and we need more leaders to speak up."

He pointed to the IPA's admirable decision to run ads

in the *Financial Times* which encouraged businesses to keep on advertising by telling them the simple truth: "When others go quiet, your voice gets louder".

Then he attempted to rally the industry with "we need to be prepared to fight".[12]

That certainly lifted my spirits. But they were soon deflated when I looked for evidence of that fight on the websites of our industry's representative organisations.

The Direct Marketing Association's site merely gave a list of demands neatly summed up by the headline: "Coronavirus: What Business Needs from Government Now".[13]

There was no mention of how direct selling could get the economy going. That was on April 25th. When I looked in mid-June, the main feature was a survey which again focused on what the government could do for the industry. In this time of crisis, JFK's "Ask not what your country can do for you . . ." sprang to mind. For there was still no evidence of an organisation that was up for a "fight".

The wrong enemy

That cannot be said of the Advertising Association. When I visited their site in April (and again in June), they were in an aggressive mood.

But the fight they were spoiling for wasn't the one that Gideon Spanier had in mind.

On the home page you had the choice of two main stories. The first was headlined: "Advertising Pays 8: UK

Advertising's Social Contribution. The Coronavirus Response".

I clicked there expecting to see a page full of the case studies that Gideon was asking for – fact after fact explaining how advertising generates growth, creates jobs, pays wages, increases tax revenues and is generally the engine of recovery whenever a spanner has been thrust into the works of UK plc's economic mechanisms.

How silly of me. The case studies were about Diversity & Inclusion; Health & Wellbeing; Community Improvement; Environmental Preservation; and Human Rights.

The second feature on the home page was headlined: "UK Advertising Needs You. Our Diversity and Inclusion Showcase".[14]

Clearly the Advertising Association's social justice warriors were not to be distracted by something as trivial as "The biggest global event since the Second World War" and its catastrophic economic impact on both UK society and the industry that their organisation was supposed to represent.

Still no reply from D&AD

As for D&AD, by the beginning of June, there was just one article "Crisis management in the time of Coronavirus: How can brands communicate effectively in times of crisis". Predictably it urged brands to "truly deliver against their purpose".[15]

Otherwise there was silence on the role the creative industries might play in dragging the country out of the impending post-pandemic recession, keeping businesses solvent and rescuing millions of families from the misery of unemployment.

So on June 2nd I sent them this email:

Hi there,

I'm being asked by an increasing number of my smaller clients to recommend books about our industry.

Do you have a reading list for such subjects as:

How to write copy that sells ... How to do effective art direction ... How to do advertising on small budgets ... How to write a brief ... How to do account planning ... How to plan media ... How to do digital advertising ... How to do SEO ... How to create a website that generates sales ... How to do effective Customer Experience.

Or any general books on how to do effective advertising in any medium?

Thanks

I got an instant "our offices are closed" message and a promise to "get back to you very shortly". As this book goes to print, they still haven't been in touch.

About a week later, a reading list did appear on D&AD's site. But it was more a recommendation on what to take on your summer staycation (those famous Pencil winners, Hilary Mantel and Naom Chomsky, for instance).

It was then taken down and replaced by a list featuring 85 books, biographies, podcasts, blogs and twitter feeds to follow if you wanted to gen up on Black Lives Matter.

One of the books I subsequently lent to the small, struggling businesses I'm helping was my edition of D&AD's classic, *The Copy Book*.

In there they'd have found a section "About D&AD"

which explained the organisation's aim to raise standards, educate people in the craft of creative communications and "increase awareness of the creative industries and the value they bring to business as well as society in general."[16]

Was that still D&AD's primary purpose? Or, as we noted in chapter 8, was it more interested in increasing awareness of the trending social justice issues of the day?

Doubling down on Purpose

It did seem that, while the rest of the country was battling for survival against Covid-19, adland was happy to keep fighting its culture wars.

When asked how the industry would look in a post Covid-19 world, Ete Davies, Chief Executive Officer at Engine, foresaw: "More work that is originated directly in response to, or out of, an increasing connection to communities and culture – with brands driven by purpose connecting behaviour and belief to help customers and see where they can play an authentically useful role, beyond just selling."[17]

Did you like that dismissive reference to "beyond just selling"?

As sales tanked, shop doors shut and the UK economy shrank by a record 20.4%, *The Drum* was running articles like: "Creative breakthrough: Can marketing truly change the world?"[18] Predictably, it began: "The modern consumer expects businesses to look beyond profit and find ways to make a meaningful stand on issues such as equality, climate change and politics."[19]

By May, *The Drum* was promoting its Can Do Festival with this blurb: "This June, the Can Do Festival will celebrate the positive energy, innovation and creative thinking that can make the marketing community such a powerful force for good."[20] Thus continuing to ignore the enormously destructive pachyderm that would be occupying the virtual conference hall.

You can bet that the "powerful force for good" the organisers had in mind had nothing to do with the fact that, pre Covid-19, every pound spent on advertising added £6 to the UK's Gross Domestic Product, that the industry contributed £120 billion to our annual GDP and was our second biggest exporting service sector generating a record £7.9 billion a year.[21]

Nor, with the onset of Covid-19, would there be any talk of making "a meaningful stand" against recession, and the suffering that the ensuing bankruptcies and unemployment would bring.

No, if there was a battle raging amongst those who Zoomed into the Can Do Festival, it would have been against the progressive left's usual demons. And those folks are hardly likely to help shore up a struggling free market economy because, for many of them, capitalism is demon #1.

Destroying capitalism

To recap on this, we have seen the disproportionate number of adlanders who identify as centre-left or left politically. In chapter 4, I said that the ad industry's anti-capitalism was evidenced by the speed and enthusiasm with which it fell in line with Extinction Rebellion.

That movement's hardcore leaders know they cannot achieve their aims unless our current economic system is destroyed. Not regulated so it will be much less carbon-reliant, nor modified to make it more sustainable. Destroyed.

Fast forward to June 2020 and the same degree of dangerous complicity could be detected in adland's reflexive, unquestioning support for Black Lives Matter.

Like environmental protection, racial equality is an inarguably just and righteous cause. But it, too, has been hijacked by hard left activists. And, in both cases, their confrontational extremism has alienated many in the mainstream who otherwise support those causes.

A quick look at UKBLM Fundraiser site tells you:"We're guided by a commitment to dismantle imperialism, capitalism, white-supremacy, patriarchy and the state structures that disproportionately harm black people in Britain and around the world."[22]

This is not boilerplate copy knocked out by some bored hack. The person who wrote it is genuine. They mean it. They aim to bring down the capitalist system. And, armed with the emotive weaponry of terms like "imperialism", "white supremacy" and "patriarchy", they'll seek to silence any moderate voices they encounter.

One of the co-founders of BLM, Patrisse Cullors, has been explicit in her aims: "Myself and Alicia [Garza] in particular have ideological frames. We are trained organisers, we are trained Marxists. We are super-versed in ideological theories."[23]

And, again let's be clear about this, the fundamental aim of those theories is the destruction of capitalism.

A convenient diversion

By now you'll have inferred that I'm not in favour of this. As Jeremy Bullmore says, "Capitalism is the least worst option we have".[24] And, as half a billion Chinese will tell you, it is very good at creating jobs, growth and wealth. Our version, with its zombie businesses, crony capitalists and huge corporate monopolies, certainly needs re-forming. But destroying, definitely not.

And, as a silent spring in Shoreditch and Soho turned to summer, the reforming had to wait. To do so at that moment would have been like changing the engines on a Boeing 747 at 35,000 feet.

As far as adlanders were concerned, the system's survival and that of their agencies, their clients, their families and their neighbours should have been the priority.

Unfortunately, in capitalism (and the UK population's) moment of dire need, the BLM furore provided left-leaning adland with a convenient diversion from the question: What part can we play in pulling the free market out of post-pandemic recession?

Convenient diversion? Well, adland is always more ideologically comfortable with questions of social justice. But, let's be honest, if we were that sincere about racial equality, then the industry could be a beacon of tolerance. But the IPA's annual Agency Census figures released in April 2020 showed that BAME participation in the industry workforce had actually fallen since the previous year. And employees of an ethnic minority background at C-suite level (4.7%) was also down.[25]

What's more, 69% of those that are BAME in adland are privately educated. Compare that to the national average of 7% and you realise we're a middle class industry to the core.[26]

On June 18th I was talking about this with James Hillhouse. He runs Commercial Break whose admirable aim is to give working class youngsters a start in the creative industries. He told me that prior to adland's sudden interest in BLM, he'd had about one inquiry a month from agencies interested in offering a job to his young talent. That's right, one a month.[27]

Closing down the conversation

We'd needed to put our elitist house in order for ages. But we chose to give it our attention at a moment that allowed capitalism's crisis to go ignored.

In fact, as adland's headline-grabbing demonstrations of enthusiasm for Black Lives Matter intensified, the conversation was closed down. And it would have been a brave person who'd even broach the subject. Or point out that unless we got the economy working again, there'd be no jobs for anyone of *any* ethnic background to go to.

No, in adland's "Marketplace of Ideas" (remember that liberal concept?) there was just one stall presenting its wares. The things being peddled were guilt and repentance, and the most valuable currency was virtue.

As such, no one wanted to talk about something as unashamedly pragmatic as pumping money back into the free market system. Especially a free market system many adlanders disliked and distrusted, and one that BLM saw as the enemy. How off-message, how inappropriate, indeed, by inference, how racist that would have been.

Hurry up and die

If anyone did mention capitalism, they were invariably against it.

Here is Dylan Williams Droga5's Chief Strategy Officer telling *Campaign* on June 3rd that "coronavirus and the failing economy" were actually "caused by the system" and "the economic model we market in our communications services".[28]

Others were keen to attack the products of that system: those narrow-minded bigots who apparently make up much of the UK population.

Mike Dowuona, the Managing Director of Crush was asked if he thought brands should shed customers who hold "disagreeable views". In his considered view: "They have a choice to make: attempt to give comfort to an ever-decreasing, ageing consumer base who revel in division by pandering to their unconscious – and sadly, in many cases, conscious – prejudice, or embrace a generation that seeks commonalities and shared experience, hence seeing a massive benefit in the long run."[29]

The basic premise being that the mainstream is irredeemably racist and should hurry up and die so that nicer, more tolerant people can take over.

The coddling of adland's mind

Again, what was missing here – and in most of the "discussions" about the causes that adland feels compelled to get involved with – was civil debate.

For example, to have someone on the article's panel challenge Dylan Williams's assertion that shareholder capitalism was the cause of Covid-19 and the subsequent recession.

Or to suggest to Mike Dowuona that what he said was itself, irredeemably racist. And that defining and stereotyping people by the apparently homogenous, negative characteristic of the group to which they belong is the very essence of racism.

Perhaps he should also have been reminded that his views would be bad for business. For example, would his Nissan client follow his advice – given that the average age of Nissan's first-time buyers is pushing 60? Aren't they exactly the people Mike wants to write off?[30]

Jonathan Haidt and Greg Lukianoff have pointed out the damage caused by this lack of diversity of opinion in their book *The Coddling of the American Mind*.[31] Their warnings are, however, going unheeded here in adland where a suffocating monoculture allows our leaders to present unchallenged opinion as incontrovertible fact.

We're kinder and more caring than we ever thought

As we've seen, nowhere has this been more apparent than in the pushing for social purpose. And, as the Covid-19 crisis deepened, its promotion gathered momentum.

There were three reasons for this.

At the best of times, individuals are reluctant to challenge adland's groupthink. It's difficult to get a hearing. And it can also be dangerous, for who wants to be cast as Piggy in the woke brigade's production of *Lord of the Flies*?

Secondly, in the first weeks of the pandemic, social purpose provided a fashionable, feel good way to fill the vacuum where the rationale for advertising's commercial purpose should have been.

Finally, its proponents looked at their own experiences of lockdown Britain and concluded that social purpose was perfectly attuned to the new mood of the people.

The industry's leaders had certainly noticed a change amongst their hard-bitten peers. Annette King, the CEO of Publicis UK felt, "we are learning how to be kinder to each other".[32] Nadja Lossgott, Executive Creative Director at AMV/BBDO, went further and said we are "more caring than you ever thought."[33] And Claire Beale, who obviously hadn't been talking to Mike Dowuona, looked forward to people coming "through it with greater empathy".[34]

As usual, adlanders projected their experience on to the nation and, in this case, concluded that the virus had had an unforeseen beneficial effect that was equivalent to a mild dose of MDMA.

Not surprisingly, this observation was used by those who push progressive projects to prove that they were, indeed, on the right side of history and the market was coming towards them.

Here's Sophie Lewis, the Chief Strategy Officer at Mcgarrybowen:"One of the fantastically positive things is we have been forced into different ways of behaving, particularly with regard to the environment, community spirit and the idea that we need to help each other, and I hope that this will persist post the virus. Brands will need to understand that better."[35]

"Turning to friends and family with warmth and good humour"

This "fantastically positive" community spirit may have been new for advertising folk. However, as Andrew Tenzer and Ian Murray's research has highlighted, the mainstream have always regarded "altruistic values such as universalism and benevolence to be important" – whereas, according to Tenzer and Murray's findings, people in adland do not.[36]

So, yes, people were looking after each other. But, if you recall Jonathan Haidt, that's only to be expected.

Remember his five foundations for moral behaviour? And how, unlike people in advertising, those in the mainstream are likely to have all of them in reasonably well balanced order.

This means that in times of social crisis those moral attributes that Haidt described as "Binding" – ie loyalty to the group, respect for authority and the ethics of community – are accentuated. Given the web of mutual obligations that, to adapt Haidt's term, bind these people, they instinctively look out for those who are close to them. Not only relatives and friends but also those who live in the houses and streets close by.

Peter Field, the IPA's guru of effectiveness noted this instinctive reaction in past recessions. During the 2008/09 financial crisis: "Our research showed that people's deeper human values were coming to the fore. As recession bit, people were responding in kind – literally – by turning to friends and family with warmth and good humour where we might have expected angst and despair."[37]

This recession's common enemy Covid-19 "has generated a level of community spirit ... that far exceeds that seen in previous recessions." The country is showing "solidarity in adversity".[38]

The numbers certainly bore that out. In April, almost half (48%) of UK adults helped someone outside their household – a remarkable increase on the 11% who'd previously reported providing a regular service or help for the sick, disabled or elderly not living with them.[39]

Community spirit in the real world

I have witnessed this myself over the past three months. While my 90-year-old asthmatic Mother has been in lockdown in Blackpool, her neighbours, Jack and Rose, have adopted her. Jack is a worldly chap whose successful joinery business took him all over the UK. To resurrect David Goodhart's typologies, whilst willing to work Anywhere, Jack is from Somewhere: the street he's lived in for over 40 years.

Since lockdown, he and Rose have taken responsibility for my Mum's wellbeing by doing her shopping, taking care of her garden and cooking her meals. They haven't become kinder. They're always like this. They are good people. They are good neighbours.

But do not think this makes them likely candidates for conversion to the causes that the social purpose advocates might try to alert them to.

If I was to ask them what they were doing about equality, diversity and climate change they would be mystified as to what might be expected of them.

Not because they are selfish or uncaring. They are the opposite of those things. But, in a town ranking third amongst those English communities that have been hardest hit by Covid-19, they have other, more immediately pressing, things to worry about – one of which is looking after my Mum.

And, as I sit here 225 miles away and unable to look after her myself, I am very grateful that they have that set of priorities – and that elderly neighbours' lives matter.

They think we're mad

If I was then to produce *Campaign* and show them this comment from Aline Santos, the Executive Vice-President of Global Marketing at Unilever: "A brand's role in culture has never been more important, because people expect us to have a point of view ... This is the time when we can see businesses and brands as the biggest healers in our society and our planet. We have to take that responsibility", Jack and Rose would look at me as if I – or Aline Santos – was mad.[40]

Now you could say we should dismiss the views of those who don't appreciate the power wielded by Aline and the corporate elite at organisations like Unilever.

But I'd point out that Jack and Rose will probably have a house full of Unilever products. It is they, and hundreds of millions like them, who keep Aline Santos in her job. And none of those people have asked Aline and her colleagues to take on the responsibility she wants Unilever to assume. In fact, most would say they don't need their moral compass setting by people who make soap and ice cream.

Like I said, Jack and Rose would think Aline Santos is bonkers. So, to explain where she is coming from, I'd summon up the shade of Mark Ritson who'd tell them: "We marketers live in a branding bubble of our creation. We think brands matter. That our brand matters. We think advertising is important. We think other people care. And with each passing year our branding bubble appears less and less transparent. An increasing number of marketers lose touch with the consumers they are meant to take their coordinates from, and fall for the bullshit that their brands and their communications make any difference to society at large and that this impact is a crucial part of their job."[41]

Advertising isn't working

Alas, Jack and Rose have got used to being ignored by out-of-touch elites.

I don't know how they vote, but Blackpool South used to be a rock solid red seat, and I imagine the two of them might have been Labour.

In the past.

But that party's commitment to divisive identity politics has alienated people like Jack and Rose – and most of the other former Labour voters on my Mum's street.

In so doing, Labour's tin-eared activists provide a salutary lesson to our industry's left-leaning proponents of purpose.

Here's campaigning socialist, Paul Embery, talking about those activists who "obsess about fringe issues in which most voters have little more than passing interest while relegating to a sideshow the everyday concerns they see as relevant to their lives ... Matters of employment, growth and prosperity can jolly well take their place behind the campaign for trans rights and Palestine in the queue for priorities."[42]

Just swap "voters" for "consumers" and you have adland's purpose-driven problem in a nutshell.

In March Andrew Tenzer, the co-author of *The Empathy Delusion,* wrote a similar piece likening the advertising industry to the Labour Party. In it he said that, like the Labour Party, we only want to talk about things we want to talk about – with people who share our views.

His article was called "Be more Tory" and the industry's trade paper, *Campaign*, refused to run it. Thus, inadvertently, proving Andrew's point.[43]

Doing what we are best at

But back to Paul Embery and his assertion that the mass of people are kept awake at night by worries about employment, growth and prosperity.

This will be especially so as the post-pandemic economic crisis deepens.

With this emergency uppermost in mind, our industry should realise that, given the two options, social purpose (saving the world) and commercial purpose (saving the economy), we can be an immediate force for good by focusing on the latter. Keeping businesses open and people in jobs is of real and practical benefit to society.

It is also a function of our core competence. It's what we are supposed to do.

The most articulate expression I've seen of this argument came from Joint Chief Strategy Officer at Abbott Mead Vickers/BBDO, Craig Mawdsley.

When we spoke, he questioned the wisdom of those clients who were happy to spend tens of millions of pounds on their purpose-driven campaigns without understanding whether they contributed to profitability or brand equity – or, ultimately, to the national exchequer.[44]

Then he sent me an article he had written that has yet to be published. For the good of the industry, it must appear in full very soon. In it, Craig acknowledged that it's quite natural for advertising people to want to make a difference and feel good about themselves.

But he pointed out that "If you're contributing to economic growth, you're doing your very best work. You're making the biggest contribution you can. You're putting your talents to their best use."[45]

How advertising should be done

However, with the economy shrinking by the hour, was anyone actually making that crucial contribution? Well, at the start of this book, I was critical of digital and how it had failed to live up to the hype that launched it back in the noughties.

I need to correct that. The industry is now the driving force of sales activation. Indeed, this is the one wing of the ad industry that's been getting products in front of the public during the current crisis.

Stephen Stretton is a Creative Director at AMV/BBDO, responsible for direct and retail work across huge clients, such as BT, Curry's and Asda: "We're doing the direct-to-consumer work and we haven't stopped throughout the lockdown. In fact, we've rarely been busier".[46]

Steve and I are from a direct marketing background, and we've been here before during the 2001 and 2008/9 recessions. But we've never known our brand-building brothers in such a petrified state.

Having said that, Steve pointed out one shining example of excellent brand work that had been done for a client he shares with Saatchi & Saatchi.

On pages 84-85, I cited BT's 1990s campaign, "It's Good to Talk", as purpose-driven advertising at its best. Well, the work they put out early in the crisis was heir to that great campaign.

In a series of 12 advertorials, the likes of Clare Balding and Fearne Cotton filled in for Bob Hoskins. And, just as Bob persuaded us to feel comfortable talking on the blower, Clare, for example, did the same thing about using WhatsApp.[47]

With "Top Tips on Tech", this was literally BT as the Enabler. And a classic example of how advertising should be done.

1) It recognised a problem faced by the prospect. 2) It expressed the solution as a consumer benefit. 3) It had a creative idea that dramatised/demonstrated that benefit.

Yes, it was all about BT's purpose. But in following the basic steps described above it persuaded rather than preached. And it had the customer's needs front and centre.

Combining brand with sales

Peter Jeavons, BT's Director of Marketing Communications spoke great sense when he explained that, compared to what other brands were saying, "What we wanted to do was almost the opposite to that – not tell people what our purpose is, but doing purposeful communications that demonstrate our purpose".

But it was also illuminating to hear him say: "We saw it as an amazing opportunity for a brand like BT to play an incredibly important role for the nation beyond trying to sell things."[48]

Illuminating because he seemed to imply that this brand building *wasn't* selling.

Of course it was. And BT is certain to see the benefit register in its bottom line in weeks, months and maybe years to come.

Hopefully others will take note, because to boost short and long term sales – and to kick start the economy – it's vital that brand building work resumes as quickly as possible.

Fortune, it appears, favours the brave.

Drawing on data from the 2009/2010 crisis, Kantar's BrandZ database said that brands that continued to invest in advertising during the last recession recovered nine times faster following it.[49] Liam Mullins at 7stars, the UK's largest media independent was even more bullish saying clients who spend will benefit from "never seen before" value in the ad market and gain a significant increase in share of voice.[50]

The most persuasive pitch was Peter Field's. If brands were to survive and then thrive during the post-pandemic recession, there had to be "a greater focus on brand advertising investment rather than on short term sales activation".

As he explained, there's a strong correlation between Share of Voice and Share of Market. And those with an

Excess Share of Voice i.e. who keep spending and see their SOV exceed their Share of Market will reap the benefits once the recession is over.

Just as importantly, those brands that don't advertise again until after the recession will take years to catch up the ground they have lost.[51]

In other words your success depends upon you maintaining your presence and them losing their nerve and pulling brand advertising spend.

Or as Mark Ritson put it in his inimitable way, "You need marketers to be shit, for your bold recession approach to succeed."[52]

You also need your advertising agency to get back to basics.

Wake up and smell Camilla's coffee

Back in April, there was little sign of that happening. But Camilla Kemp, Chief Executive of M&C Saatchi did venture this view:

"There will be an opportunity for brands not just to talk about the product, but spell out what it does for you."

Could it possibly be that she was talking about ... selling a consumer benefit?

I think she was!

However, she must have been aware of just how novel this suggestion might seem to many of her peers. So she gave a helpful example of what she meant.

"When you say to somebody, 'let's go and have a

coffee', you're not saying that because you want to consume caffeine, you're doing it because you want to connect with somebody and you want to have a moment of downtime."[53]

Got that?

Her lone voice was joined by Charlie Rudd, CEO of Leo Burnett who, with refreshing clarity, explained: "We build business by creating large customer numbers keen to buy into what the brand offers. We mobilise and persuade large groups of people to act. Populist creativity is a special power. It will be our contribution to rebuilding businesses and creating new jobs for many."[54]

Helping businesses

Unfortunately, very few ad agencies were willing to help kick-start the rebuilding process. But there were signs that those in the media industry, at least, understood the need.

In early May, Clear Channel UK offered 250 free out-of-home campaigns to local businesses. The initiative – #BusinessAsUnusual – offered 2,300+ digital six sheet posters to small High Street shops so they could drum up new trade and stay afloat.[55]

Mail Metro Media followed suit and partnered with the Federation of Small Businesses to give 1,000 small to medium-sized enterprises access to a £3million advertising fund.[56]

In a similar vein, Channel 4 offered free use of its award winning in-house team 4Creative to marketers in order to incentivise them to either resume or start advertising on TV.[57]

Of all the disciplines, media people have always had the most red-blooded approach to business. In May they could scent blood, and it was their own.

Their peers in the creative agencies were less willing to volunteer their services in order to save clients – and themselves – from bleeding out.

Tellingly, the most laudable contribution came from Harvey Austin, Alex Fearn and Dan Salkey, who'd actually been furloughed from their agency. Almost immediately, they set up Not Fur'long Creative aimed at giving marketing support to the shops, cafes and bars that lend character to the High Street. Dozens of potential clients applied for help. And, heartwarmingly, almost as many creatives, suits and planners volunteered their skills.[58]

Then, at last, one of the big agency networks pitched in when Arthur Sadoun, CEO of Publicis Groupe announced "The Pact" which promised mid-sized businesses – those with $10m to $1bn in sales and spending at least $25,000 a month in online advertising – that it would return all fees if certain KPIs weren't met.

Bob Hoffmann was cynical and called it a gimmick. But, given the need for the big networks to take some responsibility for the recovery, let's give Sadoun the benefit of the doubt.[59]

Campaign launches the fightback

Then a major breakthrough came on 15th June. Three months after the crisis began, *Campaign* came out wholeheartedly for commerce – and the crucial part advertising plays in driving it.

"The Fightback" as it was billed, started with an excellent article by Nigel Vaz, the President of the IPA, who spoke about "driving efficiency", "stimulating growth", "the business impact of ideas" and "tying creativity and communications back to business value".[60]

In short, the kind of grown-up stuff that the IPA, alone amongst the industry's representative bodies, has been talking about throughout the downturn.

Campaign then joined in with: "After the fastest downturn on record, *Campaign* believes this industry needs to restate the case for advertising as an engine of growth."

Editorial gave way to Keith Weed, the much respected former CMO of Unilever who told us: "We collectively need to make the argument that while some rules of business have been re-written during lockdown, the basic need of brand awareness and communication of brand benefits remains key for brands to drive growth ... Let's unite as an industry to show why advertising matters in building businesses and brands, the economy and jobs."

And finally there followed 11 articles by CMOs from the likes of Tesco, Centrica, Mastercard and Direct Line. By and large they repeated what Peter Field and Mark Ritson had been saying in April and May, namely that if you advertise now you'll enjoy a lasting advantage over those who don't. As Mark Ritson would have been pleased to hear, only one of them mentioned "social purpose". And that, predictably, was the person from Unilever.[61]

Dare adland use the C word?

It was all good, heartening stuff. And when I spoke with Charlie Rudd, the CEO of Leo Burnett, he gave me another reason to be cheerful.

Charlie said he'd recently detected a change of mood amongst clients. As they stared into the abyss, they realised that they needed their advertising partners as never before. And, as such, this moment of crisis was actually an opportunity for adland to prove its worth.[62]

But then, I spoiled it a bit by pointing something out about the *Campaign* feature.

Despite Keith Weed's plea that "We collectively need to make the argument" and "Let's unite as an industry to show why advertising matters", there wasn't one contribution from the leader of an advertising agency. Again, no one seemed willing to say the C word.

Perhaps they weren't invited to. But maybe, once again, we saw adland's reluctance to come out for commerce and that dirtier word, capitalism.

Was it too difficult for a predominantly left-leaning community to make that case? And more to the point, dare anyone do it.

Let me put that question in context. The bulk of that edition of *Campaign* was given over to the industry's response to Black Lives Matter which, let's not forget, is a movement devoted to the destruction of capitalism.

On what had been turned into the ultimate binary issue, who would want to risk being accused of reading from a different page and having other priorities? As BLM has it: "silence is violence". At that moment, for adland, you might have added: "stray out of the bubble and you could be in trouble."

Even we don't believe in purpose

What, then, would it take for the advertising industry to openly champion the cause of commerce and competitive persuasion? And what, in this time of crisis, might get its spokesmen and women to dial down their emphasis on social purpose?

Maybe the answer came on June 24th when Andrew Tenzer and Ian Murray published *The Aspiration Window* – their latest investigation into the behavioural, attitudinal and psychological differences between advertising and marketing and the mainstream.[63]

Once again they found that adland is so far removed from the real world that its orbiting bubble can be seen only with the most powerful telescope. However, this time round, they did find one point at which they intersected.

If the mainstream is not influenced by a brand's stance on political and social issues, it appears that we're not that bothered either.

First, mainstream samples were asked what factors are

important to them in making purchase decisions. In that research, just 1 in 10 said 'a brand's position on social issues' or 'political stance and affiliations' played a role in their buying decisions.

Advertisers and marketers were then asked the same question. Less than 3 in 10 made reference to "concern for environmental issues" when buying, and less than 2 in 10 consider other social virtue factors such as "position on social issues" and "political stance and affiliations".

The important factors were pretty much the same for both samples.

As Tenzer and Murray concluded: "The inconvenient truth for social virtue advocates is that even at the height of the Covid-19 crisis, it's good old fashioned attributes like value for money, reliability, product and service and customer service that are top priorities for the mainstream and for advertising and marketers too.[64]

"We have identified a clear disconnect between one of the dominant narratives in our industry and practitioners' beliefs about what actually works. The simple fact is that even people in the industry don't believe social virtue matters to mainstream audiences. We believe the industry probably champions it to make it feel better about itself."[65]

If adlanders continue to do so then they may be able to pride themselves on being on the right side of history. However, as Ian Murray suggested: "The empathy and aspiration gap that persists between marketers and the mainstream means it's too easy for brands to end up on the wrong side of the conversation."[66]

"We want to be unashamed about what we do."

But would the extreme proponents of purpose ever accept this? Or would they resist, disparage and sabotage attempts to sell our way out of the crisis the old fashioned way?

Perhaps what was needed was an agency that didn't have to appease such people. And one whose primary purpose was building brands and selling products.

Enter James Murphy, David Golding and Ian Heartfield – and their start-up: New Commercial Arts.

The first two had been the driving force behind Adam & Eve/DDB. They'd won *Campaign's* Agency of the Year award six times in just 10 years and, not surprisingly, were the magazine's Agency of the Decade. To top that, in June, 2020, they were also named "Europe's Agency of the Decade" at Cannes.

When the golden couple, Murphy and Golding, resigned in 2019, adland waited impatiently to see what they'd turn their prodigious talents to next.

What they'd done was spot a gap in the market. Make that two.

The first was a disconnect between brand building and customer experience. NCA was going to merge the two to create brand building comms from the top of the funnel to the bottom.

But, most interestingly, Murphy and Golding had noticed something more fundamental about adland. It had stopped selling – and lost its way.

Here's how Murphy saw things:

"We want to be unashamed about what we do. It seems

that our industry has been slightly ashamed of what it does in recent years and it's been flailing around trying to articulate its role. Our name very deliberately has the word commercial because that is what our industry does. We'll help build brands and make successful businesses, and that's what commercial arts is there to do."

He then used a term I'd not come across in nine months of researching and writing this book. Indeed, I said I'd been looking in vain for it way back on page seven.

Murphy talked about striving to get "a much higher conversion to sale".[67]

Hallelujah!

If the most successful advertising man in the industry was talking about "conversion to sale" and making "brands more desirable and easier to buy", then could a corner have been turned?[68]

Appealing to the mainstream

It was even more encouraging to hear that his creative partner, Ian Heartfield, wanted to appeal to the mainstream audience that adland had lost touch with. "I really want us to make work that people see or experience in the real world. There's a bit of a bubble at the moment, there's an awards lens on that. And what I want to do is make work *everybody* loves. I want my cousins in the Isle of Wight and family across the country to love and see the work. For it to be talked about at bus stops and water coolers."[69]

To do this, he'll have to build the kind of diverse team that the industry so lacks. By that, I mean looking beyond the bubble and hiring from what Heartfield referred to as "the real world". Those who share the values of his cousin in the Isle of Wight. Who harbour the same aspirations as the workers who queue for the bus each morning. And who understand the communitarian values that Jack and Rose have built their lives upon.

If they pull that off, and if their focus on brand building and selling is successful, there'll be hope for all.

Until then, we need more individuals like Tom Roach. On the day before Tenzer and Murray presented *The Aspiration Window*, he called his latest blog post: "Brand Purpose: The biggest lie the industry ever told?". Tom, who has won numerous effectiveness awards at such great agencies as AMV, BBH and Adam & Eve/DDB wrote:

"What we *really* need to do is prove our value to society, to prove our *commercial* value first and foremost – to have pride in the value we create and so demonstrate the role we play in driving the economy, and therefore society, forwards. There's plenty of genuine virtue to be had in that."[70]

Unfortunately, these wise words only appeared on Tom's blog. Such alternative views have to be amplified by our industry's representative bodies, its leaders and the trade press.

And quickly.

Adland's leaders must speak out

As I send this three month survey of the industry's response to Covid-19 to the publisher, the newsfeeds make for grim reading. Keir Starmer has warned of 3 million unemployed.[71] According to the Organisation for Economic Cooperation and Development, that's a conservative estimate. They say we could be looking at five million, and an unemployment rate of 14.8%, the highest since 1932.[72]

Here's the fight that adland should be waging: the war on unemployment. Because social justice starts with a job and the means of providing for yourself and your family. And the poorest will need our help here more than anyone because they have no savings to fall back on and no nepotism network to open doors for them. Indeed, the ones who already face discrimination will be the first to have those doors slammed shut upon them.

We need everyone from Stephen Woodford at the Advertising Association to Stephen Lepitak at *The Drum*. From Cilla Snowball at AMV/BBDO to Kate Stanners at D&AD. From Marc Lewis at the School of Communication Arts to Mark Read at WPP to speak up. The industry's influential figures must exercise the privilege of power to tweet, blog and talk about adland's crucial role in the UK's fight for economic survival.

On page 146, I quoted from an, as yet, unpublished article by Craig Mawdsley. I said then that for the good of the industry the trade press needs to publish it soon.

I can think of no better way to finish a book about why

advertising has to rediscover its commercial purpose than to quote from that article. In so doing I might even reconcile some of the more pragmatic proponents of social purpose to the cause of selling.

"Your skills lie in helping to grow businesses and make people more prosperous. You're really good at that. And you should feel really good about it. Because every fraction of every percentage point you add to GDP growth lifts people's incomes, enables more money to be spent on education, funds medical research and helps treat disease. By making more money for everyone, you're helping make the world a better place for everyone."[73]

11
Advertising's Somewheres speak out

Welcome back.

The last bit that you read came out in the summer 2020. It's now June 2021. So what's happened in between?

Let's start with the dog that didn't bark (or, for that matter, bite)

When the book was published, I expected to be savaged by a culturally left-leaning ad industry.

Indeed I'd joined the WPP (no, not that one) and was set to move into a safe house where no one from the big agencies could ever find me (i.e. anywhere outside the M25).

But before I went into hiding, I wanted people to know about the book. So I broke the habits of a lifetime and posted something on Twitter.

And got more notifications than I knew I had followers.

To my amazement, all were supportive.

It was the same with LinkedIn.

I assumed once the advocates of social purpose got wind of this, they'd rally and the counter attack would be vicious.

Again, nothing.

And the more positive feedback I received, the more I realised I'd been wrong about one big thing.

I'd assumed that the entire industry was sold on purpose.

Far from it.

Advertising's Somewheres find their voice

The first thing that struck me was the vigorous support I was getting from agencies outside London.

Andy Bunday, Creative Director at The&Partnership in Manchester, wrote: "To everyone working in what's left of our business: I'd like to ram this book so far down your throat that you could read it without taking your head out of your arse. Steve H nails modern agencies. To a cross."[1]

This amused his counterparts in Newcastle and Bristol, Leeds and Glasgow. The inference being that the people executing the unusual yoga position Andy described were running the "modern agencies" down in London.

Also from Manchester, but a little more measured, was this from Justine Wright, the founder and Managing Director of Cuckoo Design.

"I started my career at one of the big network agencies where we would spend days writing briefs, I had no idea how much time had been spent on a job, nobody told me what worked and what didn't work. I moved to a small agency and from day one I was taught about results and commerciality. It never left me. I now own the agency and we are still going strong. We are all about driving sales for our clients, making a realistic margin and providing a great place to work."[2]

In their scorn and scepticism, Andy and Justine speak for advertising's Somewheres.

These regional shops are staffed largely by local talent, to service local businesses and sell to local people. And, guess what? This local knowledge is a big advantage.

Sarah Mason, formerly a Planning Director at VCCP and

now Head of Planning at S3 Advertising in Cardiff says: "It is so much easier to empathise with the audience we usually have to reach because the agency is embedded in the community. We go home to the people we're selling to every evening and mix with them at the weekend."

Shops like Sarah's know how effective their creative work is – and needs to be. With clients who look for a return on the money they've invested in their advertising – and check the figures on a daily basis – they still live by David Ogilvy's motto, "We Sell – Or Else".

As Sarah told me, "They are very focused on the result, believe me. And that means we are too. If we don't hit their targets, we might not get paid!"[3]

The regional agencies are entrepreneurs dealing with entrepreneurs. Of necessity, they've never given up on their commercial purpose. And it seems my book offered some vindication for – and indeed celebration of – the way they'd stuck to their knitting, regardless of how unfashionable the pattern they were working to might be.

Who gives a crap?

But what of the ones who set and follow fashion? I'm talking about those who work in London's creative agencies for big corporate clients. As Justine Wright found, many who work on these accounts have little knowledge of or interest in the success or failure of their efforts.

Vanessa Morrish, Head of Creative and Brand at Who

Gives A Crap, the Australian-based, D&AD award-winning eco-toilet paper company recently reminisced about her days as an art director with Iris, London when "we were sheltered from the metrics. It never occurred to me that work should be effective".[4]

I'm sure she spoke for many others today who couldn't give a shit whether their work works. And why should they? They are so insulated from the realities of business that, until recently, it's unlikely they'd be fired, reprimanded or even informed if their last ad bombed

Naturally, I didn't expect to get much support for a return to a results-based commercial purpose from these folks.

However, as I said, the initial shitstorm never broke. In fact, I started to build a following amongst these adlanders.

Too scared to speak out

How did I know? Well, from September onwards I popped a regular post on LinkedIn, each of which drew anything from 5,000 to 13,000 views.

According to my dashboard, dozens came from the likes of Ogilvy, M&C Saatchi, AMV/BBDO, Adam & Eve/DDB, Wunderman Thompson, Iris, Publicis Sapient, VMLY&R, Havas, BBH, McCann Worldgroup and VCCP.

I expected these people to offer the strongest disagreement. Yet the one dissenting voice came from Toby Allen, Deputy ECD at AMV/BBDO and lead creative on *Viva la Vulva.* He wrote in to say that "Agencies have a huge role to play in advocating substantive purpose as a future proof commercial strategy".[5]

We then had a good debate about whether you can "future proof" any strategy. However, aside from his understandable desire to have his two penneth (see pages 46-48 and 90), there was nothing from his peers.

Which, by inference, meant they weren't moved to disagree.

But in the dozen or so posts I put out, only five people from London's leading creative agencies made supportive comments. Even fewer clicked on "Like".

So the silence that greeted the posts hinted at the lack of opposition. Which, for my part, was good.

But, ominously, that silence also spoke volumes about adland's fear of openly supporting my argument.

12
The clique that's setting adland's agenda

To understand why people are generally reluctant to comment, we must realise that the bandwagon of social purpose is now a juggernaut – and no one wants to get crushed under its wheels or, worse still, thrown beneath them.

In the driving seat are a coterie of individuals who wield a disproportionate degree of power within the industry.

Firstly there are the careerists who've clambered to the top by supporting inarguably worthy causes. We all know leaders who are three parts ECD and two parts SJW. They owe their success to the personal brand they've built around that carefully cultivated duality.

Nowadays, it's not enough to have an IPA Effectiveness Award-winning campaign in your book. You need to show you've started a charity supporting a D&I initiative, or you're an ever-present on the climate crisis speaking circuit.

I have spoken to half a dozen senior creatives who tell me they've been "let go" or overlooked for jobs because they don't have the kind of credentials mentioned above. As one described it, "the optics" weren't correct. He meant he didn't look right i.e. he's white, male and over forty.

Another said that, in his final six months at a network agency production house, he was given just one directing job: the task of rescuing a commercial that had been shot by an inexperienced young female director. After which it was he, not she, who got fired.

Sadly but understandably, those individuals have asked me not to attribute their comments. They want to have at least a half chance of getting the next job they go for.

This discrimination on the basis of age and gender goes right to the top of the job market. A senior suit at Ogilvy tells me that when Andy Main was lured from Deloitte Digital to become the network's Global CEO, there was a collective cultural cringe.

Back in the 1990s Ogilvy had thrown a brick through the glass ceiling by appointing Charlotte Beers and then Shelly Lazarus to the top jobs. Was this now a retrograde step? Surely another woman or, better still, a person of colour would have been more appropriate.

No doubt mindful of this, Main used his opening address to emphasise the commitment to "a clear culture of belonging, where talented people from under-represented groups are championed and supported throughout their careers, and given the chance to reach the very highest levels of the organisation."[1]

Admirable stuff. But not very reassuring for one group of talented under-represented individuals. If it's true that David Ogilvy didn't begin his career as copywriter until he was pushing forty, he'd have little chance today of getting a start at his own agency.

The activists who impose that agenda

If the careerists use progressive causes to make themselves marketable, activists use the industry's institutions to market the agenda.

For them, the ends justify the dodgy means. For example last November the D&AD Chairman, Tim Lindsay, admitted that Pencils are given to purpose-driven work that "undoubtedly is a scam".[2]

Worse still, the head of the advertising world's most august awards body believes that "green wash and woke washing is actually a step in the right direction". This despite the fact that John Sauven, Executive Director of Greenpeace UK, has spoken out against these scams. "This is a golden age for greenwash," he told the *Financial Times* a couple of weeks after Tim made his comment. "Any company that wants to gain the public's trust and be a genuine green leader needs to put in the hard work first and put up the billboards later."[3]

On the subject of trust Alan Jope, CEO of Unilever, had already warned, "Woke washing is beginning to infect our industry. It's polluting purpose. It's putting in peril the very thing which offers us the opportunity to help tackle many of the world's issues. What's more, it threatens to further destroy trust in our industry, when it's already in short supply."[4]

Jope is right to worry. Last November's Ipsos MORI poll showed that people who work in advertising are now the least trusted collective in the UK. We came bottom in a list of 30, ranking below bankers, politicians and estate agents.[5]

So the fact that an industry leader believes we have the moral authority to lecture (and then mislead) the public beggars belief.

But, when it comes to (a)moral authority, the people now running D&AD feel they have the right to impose theirs on all of us.

In October, the organisation got a new President in

Naresh Ramchandani. By way of introduction, Tim Lindsay said Naresh is a "strong believer in making the right ethical choices for our industry."[6]

No one in the industry has asked him to make those moral choices on their behalf, but having no mandate doesn't seem to bother either Naresh or Tim.

History tells us it's never a great idea to allow this kind of responsibility to fall to people whose views lie on the extreme of the mainstream. But that's what we're getting with D&AD.

Its new President has stated "that brands need to be politically-minded", and it is clear which end of the political spectrum Naresh expects them to occupy.[7]

For his part, Tim now defines good work as producing "better outcomes" not merely in traditional commercial terms, but also "socially, culturally, politically, environmentally."[8] As we're about to see, if you're hoping to win one of the D&AD's awards, you'd best ensure your own views on social, cultural, political and environmental issues conform to Tim's.

Cancel culture comes to adland

Most people know about D&AD because of those awards. On its website section headlined:"Where does the money I spend on my entries go?" it says: "What people often don't realise is that D&AD is a charity. In fact, everything we do is about inspiring the next generation of creative talent, improving their access to the industry, and nurturing and developing their skills."[9]

Which is how they justify charging up to $1,458 plus VAT an entry.

But that isn't how Naresh, the new President, wants to spend it.

As D&AD's website explained: "During his tenure, Ramchandani will work with D&AD and the board of trustees to investigate how creativity can tackle global issues, and will explore how the sector can help combat climate change by amplifying environmental protest and sustainable practice."[10]

The aim is to further politicise the organisation and then the industry – and to use not only the income from the competition but also the awards themselves as the main tool for achieving that.

In a podcast aired a few weeks after Naresh's arrival, Tim Lindsay and copywriter Ben Kay, suggested that D&AD "start awarding or witholding Pencils on the basis of the diversity of cast and crew".[11]

Which means that initially, creative excellence will be secondary to quotas set by D&AD's self-appointed guardians of Diversity & Inclusion. And thereafter, the credits for most of the work that wins a Pencil will be a testimony to tickbox tokenism.

It was also mooted that "in five years' time or ten years' time we'll look back and go 'petrol driven car advertising or companies like that shouldn't have been awarded.'"[12]

So cancel culture comes to adland. And all the exemplary work that won a Pencil for VW, Volvo or BMW etc will be morally downgraded and, by inference, those who did it regarded as collaborators in crimes against the environment.

And finally if, in the past, there have been categories for "ethical work" then that means "the norm is unethical". Following that logic, in future it will be best if "the central D&AD and everything else is ethical" with the "unethical" stuff being marginalised.

Applying a deft use of doublespeak, Tim said "The aim is to normalise the right kind of behaviour" i.e. by making sure the vast majority of Pencils are awarded to work with a social purpose strategy.[13]

Here again we see the "controlling and dogmatic" left-brain thinking we noted on page 102 and which Orlando Wood so brilliantly exposed and explained in his book *Lemon*.[14] Because, with "normalise" what Tim really means is that he and his fellow activists are going to impose their politicised groupthink upon an entire industry – and, by extension, the UK public who'll be exposed to the subsequent advertising.

Groupthink

Actually, as we all know, groupthink is already dominant. And the problem is, no one challenges it.

Indeed it's a great irony that an industry that puts such emphasis on diversity appears to be so lacking in diversity of opinion.

In August 2020, the BBH Strategist Harry Guild made this point when he analysed the relative likemindedness of those involved in Marketing, Law, Teaching, IT and five other occupations.

As he concluded: "Looking at cohesion by profession,

Marketing is by far the most like-minded industry that TGI measures. This is advertising's biggest problem in a single chart. This is the monoculture . . . We like to style ourselves as free thinkers, mavericks and crazies, but the grim truth is that we're a more insular profession than farming and boast more conformists than the military."[15]

It's a poor reflection on our industry. But what's even more disturbing is that this conformity of thought and opinion is being enforced from within.

The new religion

As I pointed out on pages 66-67, our universities provide the industry with a hard core of recruits versed in the new religion of social justice.

Like all devout believers, they take comfort in the monodirectional certainty their faith provides.

Underpinning this faith is the ideology that has dominated UK academia for the past 20 years, critical theory. While few actually read its gospels according to Lukacs and Adorno, Foucault and Derrida, Bell and Crenshaw; many believe in its trinity of grievances – namely that society is systemically racist, sexist and homophobic.

At university its ardent followers are allowed to close down debate and intimidate those who do not share either their views or those of their progessive tutors.

In November 2020, Survation research indicated that 44% of students reckoned their tutors would treat them differently if they openly expressed their opinions, 38%

said speaking up would adversely damage their careers and 36% of students held views that, while legal to express, would be considered unacceptable by their student union.[16]

Dave Trott takes up their story:"At university, we learn our purpose is to educate the world to a woke agenda. It's a noble quest and anything else is ignorant and stupid. We bring this into advertising and believe that is the whole purpose of our job."[17]

There's little willingness to either debate an alternate point of view, or accept the legitimacy of one that differs from their own.

Rory Sutherland sounded an early warning of the effect this new fundamentalism would have on the industry. Three years ago, he wrote: "You can have a brilliant reputation and have earned the respect of the industry and peers. But one sentence in a speech you made six months ago in Belgrade can be held against you and instantly destroy your career."[18]

Rory was right. And now there's a tension abroad in London's adland and, indeed, a fear of being cancelled for voicing an unconventional belief or opinion.

For example, one senior figure tells me they have to keep their strong Christian belief to themself. They feel that to do otherwise would jeopardise any chance of promotion. Another told me how they'd been physically accosted for saying something that deviated slightly from the party line on diversity.

Bosses are scared – and silent

Confronted by the absolutes of the woke worldview, agency bosses remain silent on such fundamental matters as the main reason everyone turns up for work each day. Which, whisper it, is to help their clients make a healthy profit by selling things.

I spoke to one CEO of a global network who said the pressure to remain quiet in face of the politicisation of the workplace was now almost unbearable.

Some CEOs have taken the path of least resistance and started preaching the social justice gospel themselves.

But in ceding control in this way, they have not only abandoned their staff to the new Inquisition but also made themselves vulnerable. The agency Torquemadas have been brought up to believe that freedom of expression is a false consciousness and all power derives from patriarchal privilege.

For them, the root of all evil is, of course, capitalism and the representatives of the white male patriarchy who preside over the system – and over the ad agencies and networks where these zealots work.

As such, they have scant respect for the authority of those who manage the business. In fact, they feel empowered to remove anyone by simply accusing them of an heretical comment, gesture or decision.

As I said, allowing extremists to fix your moral compass isn't a great idea. But, that's what's happening in London's adland (and in so many of the UK's institutions and industries). And, as we await the arrival of our own

Savonarola, no one dares speak out for fear of having their CV burned on a bonfire in Hoxton Square.

Crisis? What crisis?

In this febrile atmosphere, it's understandable why my argument got muted support from London's leading agencies. I sense that those who are sympathetic are tired of politics intruding into their work life. On page 99, we saw research by the More in Common Community, created in memory of murdered Labour MP Jo Cox, which found that the vast majority of people "share a sense of fatigue with our polarised national conversation."

I imagine that many adlanders feel the same way. They want to get on with their job. But they know that if they want to keep it, they'd best keep schtum.

Added to which, when my book came out in August 2020, my emergency appeal for the industry to use its commercial skills to get the economy working again was easy to ignore.

The relaxing of lockdown restrictions which began in June started a summer bounceback and optimistic talk of a V-shaped recession.

The shops were open, the pubs were full, and the beaches – be they in Bournemouth or Bodrum – beckoned.

True, something like one in 10 people in marketing had lost their job.[19] But at the big London agencies, Chancellor Rishi Sunak's furlough cash was keeping the P45s at bay.

So why worry? Or, indeed, why challenge the new faith and make that sacrilegious shift from social to commercial purpose when all seemed reasonably well with the world?

Alas that feeling of wellbeing was inspired by a dead cat bounce. And the UK's third quarter recovery proved weaker than that of both the eurozone and the US.

A stricter, longer initial lockdown was one obvious cause. But underlying that was the UK economy's over-dependence on the mainstream audience getting their debit cards out and spending. As the *Financial Times* pointed out, the feeble UK rebound was a result of "weak household consumption compared with other countries."[20]

To highlight the message, the House of Commons Treasury Select Committee paper *What are the challenges to economic recovery from coronavirus?*, published on September 11th, led with:"Recovery of Consumption – The Problem."[21]

Professor Andy Haldane, Chief Economist at the Bank of England, said the way back would be dependent upon "for want of a better word, animal spirits on the part of both businesses and households, in terms of their willingness to spend in the face of what is still a very significant cloud of uncertainty with high exposure to the retail and hospitality sectors."[22]

According to the Institute of Fiscal Studies, those households had plenty to spend, for they had saved a record 28.1% of income during the second quarter – roughly three to four times more than normal.[23]

The market was there. But where were the marketers?

Alas the only person in the industry who openly argued for adland to take the lead and drive demand was Nigel Vaz, President IPA and CEO Publicis Sapient.

On September 15th he wrote: "At this crucial time, the government should be partnering with the advertising industry in shared endeavour: to kick-start the economy by boosting consumer spending and fuelling growth."[24]

At first glance, it was encouraging to see *Campaign* airing such an unfashionable view. Then it became apparent this wasn't in there because the industry trade paper thought it worthy of coverage. This was a "promotional" piece. The IPA had to pay for the privilege of reminding the industry of its crucial role in a time of national crisis.

A couple of weeks later, *Campaign* gave us a more accurate insight into where its head was at.

13
Diversity – has adland missed the point?

In October's edition, *Campaign's* Deputy Editor, Gemma Charles reminded us that BLM was the "other defining issue of 2020".[1]

As we've seen, the industry threw itself whole-heartedly behind the Black Lives Matter protests – and began a bout of very public repentance and recrimination about its prejudiced past.

Sure enough, BLM made the industry feel very guilty, especially given the political leanings of those who work there. How shameful that people so committed to social justice should have their own failings highlighted.

In truth, it was a fair cop. We saw on page 81 that the industry draws its recruits from the university-educated middle classes. And that includes the BAME personnel. As Wieden + Kennedy's Head of Planning and brilliant blogger, Martin Weigel says, having "a somewhat more diverse bunch of toffs really isn't going to change that much."[2]

When, in summer, the Brixton Finishing School polled its graduates and applicants on the barriers to entry into the industry, the headlines were made by those 31% who cited race as the main obstacle.

But over twice as many (71%) said "not knowing the right people" was the biggest problem.[3] The "right people" are, of course, the scions of middle class parents. Nepotism and networking gets them a place in London's agencies. And keeps the working classes out.

Is class a bigger barrier than race?

The two former comprehensive school boys, Anthony Hopper and Simon Goodall, who now run their consultancy, The Ninety-Niners, nailed it when they said "the industry says it's a meritocracy but it takes money and influence just to get in the room." They'd seen too many new recruits who "owed their place to parents who knew someone who worked in the agency. Or whose parents actually worked in the industry and had groomed them for a role."[4]

In their view, if you're not from that class and don't have those connections, you have less chance.

Indeed, if we discriminate then, as Reach Research has indicated, it is more likely to be by class than skin colour. They asked "When you think of 'people like me' what aspects of yourself do you consider?"

Respondents replied "Age" 47% and "Social class" 44%.

They were followed by "Life stage" and "Income" – which are variants on age and class.

As for "Ethnicity", it ranked seventh in importance at 22%.[5]

So if a subconscious bias leads us to hire in our own image, it's little wonder that advertising is one of the most ageist industries in the UK and, in the words of that great (working class) art director, Dave Dye, there are "too many Jolyeons and not enough Bobs".[6]

Anthony and Simon, cited above, told me that on their first day at work their public school educated boss asked "How on earth did you get in here?" when he found out which school they went to.[7]

Nick Myers, Head of Planning at Oliver, had a similar experience. When, in the early days of his career, he went for an interview at J Walter Thompson he was asked: "Well, I know which school you went to and I know the postcode you live in, so why should I hire you?"

Nick was born in Birmingham of West Indian parents. He has had to live with colour being a barrier. He also knows that if he went for a job with a rich Brummie accent he'd have more difficulty. However, with a rich plummy accent he'd probably be OK.[8]

As we noted on page 137, 69% of the industry's BAME people are privately educated. As such, when they went for their first job, the person interviewing them just saw "someone like me".

Adland's quick fix

Ally Owen, who runs the Brixton Finishing School, drew on her own experience as a working class creative in a predominantly middle class area. "Only 5% of our industry is working class," she says, "when 30% of the population is. I live near Dalston, which is full of all types of wonderful people, but the odds of seeing any of my neighbours in my workspaces ..."[9]

Ally was talking about working class people from *all* backgrounds. And this is where the long-term focus should be.

But adland, in its reflexive response to BLM, rushed out a pledge to fight "'systemic inequality' within the industry and support Black talent."[10]

As a result, Nick Myers says he foresees "an influx of that Black talent at the lower levels but I fear that cultural and class barriers mean few will break through to the upper echelons of the agency world."The unconscious or, as we saw from Nick's experience and that of Anthony and Simon, fully conscious bias of the middle class elite means "the new recruits' progress will remain an uphill struggle."[11]

James Hillhouse, who we first met on page 137, says Nick's fears are well-founded.

His company, Commercial Break, has been trying to get working class youngsters into the creative industries for the past decade. James recently asked those who'd got jobs with ad agencies what their experiences had been like. Most said the same thing. Initially great excitement on their part. And a very warm welcome from the agency. Then, nothing. No training, no progression plan and no realisation by the agency that there was a cultural disconnect between them and the newcomers. In most cases it was left to the recruits to adapt or leave.

As James says, "it takes honesty, commitment and time to make the relationship work."[12] Unfortunately the ad industry, with its short attention span and its fixation with fads and fashion, hasn't the patience required to solve "systemic" problems systematically. Opening up its doors is fine, but devising plans for training, progression, and acculturation programmes takes time to organise – and even longer to deliver results.

So, confronted by the dismal lack of Black people actually planning, creating and directing the commercials, and unable to quickly achieve the quotas they'd like to set themselves, agencies projected them onto the nation's TV screens.

By early autumn it seemed there was a Black or mixed race actor/actress in every other commercial. As Bayo Furlong Co-Director of The Eye Casting, commented: "When was the last time we saw a brief that didn't have a mixed-race couple in it?"[13]

It was time, apparently, for advertising to truly reflect the make-up of the UK population.

Problem was, it didn't.

What's wrong with this picture?

This was the world as seen by adlanders who live in one of the most international and ethnically mixed cities in the world. And yes, Black people do make up 15% of London's population. However, according to GovUK statistics, updated in August of last year, Black people account for 3.3% of the UK population.[14]

Which means, the vision of UK society presented in the ads must have puzzled many white viewers. For it showed a picture quite different from the world in which they live.

For example, in the last census of my home town, Blackpool, Black people made up 0.2% of the population.[15] It might well have edged up since then. But in my most recent trip in April, I didn't see one Black person in the seven days I was up there. And, believe me, this isn't because Blackpool is a middle class haven of white privilege. In fact, you might have difficulty explaining the concept of "white privilege" to people who live in a town that has eight out of the ten most deprived neighbourhoods in England, and the lowest life expectancy in the country.[16]

This is not a selective snapshot either. As Ben Walker pointed out in *The New Statesman* in June 2020, "Britain's ethnic minorities are concentrated in England, almost entirely in a select few towns and cities, such as London, Birmingham, Luton and the urban conurbations straddling West Yorkshire and Greater Manchester. A white person could grow up on the coast of Yorkshire, just two hours away from one of the most diverse cities in the region, and have next to no interaction with someone of a different ethnicity."

He added: "Ethnic minorities make up more than 30% of the population in Bradford and Blackburn, for example, but more than half of neighbourhoods in both places remain more than 85% white".[17]

Unfortunately but inevitably, there was a reaction from those who objected to what they saw as a distorted picture. For example, the Sainsbury's Christmas commercial, *Gravy Song* which featured a Black family, was trolled on Twitter and YouTube by people complaining that they "did not see themselves in the ad".[18]

How to piss everybody off

Ironically, when it came to content rather than casting, angry whites were joined by equally angry Blacks. Some critics accused adland of blithely reinforcing stereotypes. Others said the agencies were merely casting Black actors in roles that could have been played by white people.

Like their white counterparts, they did not see themselves in the ads.

Research commissioned by Channel 4 found that nearly two thirds (62%) of BAME people said that advertising did not represent Black and brown cultures well.[19]

There was a lack of authenticity and little attempt to reflect the wide range of lived experience in the very varied and diverse Black, Asian and Minority Ethnic sectors of society.

True enough, but if anyone had the right to say that, it was those from the Asian community which makes up 6.8% of the UK population.

In 2019 the biggest ever study into diversity in TV advertising looked at 1,000 commercials shown in the UK over a two-month period. It revealed that some 37% featured Black people, of which 13% showed a Black person in the lead.

Conversely, those from South Asia appeared in just 8% of ads and took the lead role in only 3%.[20]

This discrepancy was also seen in TV programming.

In October 2020, the Creative Diversity Network Report found that, as in advertising, while BAME talent is sorely missing behind the camera, it is "overrepresented" in front of it. This exposure, however, is not uniform.

People from BAME backgrounds accounted for more than 22% of all on-screen TV contributions last year, while representing 12.8% of the UK population. But over the past three years, on-screen contributions by South Asian ethnic groups have fallen from 7.1% to 5.6%.[21]

In wake of the BLM protests, the gap between Black and Asian representation is certain to have widened. So, it seems that in programming, as in advertising, when it comes to casting, Black lives matter a little bit more than brown lives.

But what of that other neglected ethnic minority, the white working class? Well the only time you see them in an ad is when diamond geezers like Harry Rednapp and Ray Winstone invite members of their tribe to blow that week's meagre wages at BetVictor or Bet 365.

As the UK's leading political pollster Deborah Mattinson shows in *Beyond the Red Wall*, they already feel "such a powerful collective sense of grievance" over the way they are treated by the metropolitan elites.[22] And a major source of anger is the diet they are force fed by those who control the media. For example, only 37% of C2DE adults trust the BBC to tell the truth, and many have simply stopped watching its programmes.[23]

Does it matter to adland that we present an inaccurate picture of the composition of UK society? Or that we misrepresent our Black citizens and largely ignore those from the Asian community and white working class?

I doubt it. But what is clear is that in our rush to atone for our sins and display our commitment to our version of diversity, adland has blundered into the minefield of race relations. And, in so doing, may well have made them more explosive.

14
Fit for purpose?

If adland's thought leaders fell over themselves to take the knee, they bowed to no one in their commitment to social purpose.

Or in their acceptance that every performative gesture was an act of game-changing altruism.

Even the most dubious claims about a brand's ability to right society's wrongs went unquestioned. For example, back in September 2019, *The Drum* reproduced Cadbury Dairy Milk's announcement that it would be working with Age UK to "solve old-age loneliness."[1]

With a sickly confection of marketing speak and sanctimony, a brand spokesperson said: "We are encouraging people to find their glass & a half of kindness and generosity and donate their [words] through small gestures that could really help change the lives of older people."[2]

The *We've donated our words* campaign ended in February 2020. That's right, just as Covid-19 and the real ordeal for millions of elderly people was about to begin. Here, if ever there was one, was the ideal moment for the brand to make a crucial contribution.

Yet from then until September, it fell silent.

The brand's partner, Age UK actually published a report on October 16, 2020 describing how millions had "suffered devastating levels of anxiety" between March and September.[3]

By then Cadbury Dairy Milk had finally responded. This time it was *Campaign's* turn to reprint the press release, telling us that "Cadbury celebrates older people by finding out fun stories from their past – Film by VCCP encourages people to talk about adventurous and romatic (sic 1) aspects of life, instead of focusing on pratical (sic 2) concerns."[4]

Clearly Cadbury had tired of such "practical concerns" as "devastating levels of anxiety". Just as the UK's aged population descended into a long, dark autumn and winter of solitary confinement, and physical and mental enfeeblement, client and agency decided it was time for a bit of "fun".

And to incentivise this latest outbreak of Cadbury's-style "kindness and generosity", they were even willing to run a prize draw for a hamper full of chocolate worth one hundred pounds!

So, job done then.

Meanwhile, in the real world, a story of lasting significance was emerging from the Cadbury/Mondelez camp. During Dairy Milk's silent summer of 2020, a lot of hard work went into bringing production of the chocolate back from factories in Europe to Bourneville, Birmingham.

It was applauded by all political parties and prompted Joe Clarke, of the Unite trade union to say: "To complete consultations and negotiations to deliver this fantastic investment, even in the midst of the Covid restrictions, is a credit to the trade union representatives, the members and the business."[5]

For the local workforce and their families this really was an enduring force for good. But it didn't come with a 60 second film on YouTube and a hyperbolic press release. So the UK advertising and marketing journalists decided it wasn't worth donating any of their words to.

"No merit in profit without purpose"

That Dairy Milk example wasn't an aberration. As each week went by, a new CMO or ECD took their own deep dive into the shallow end of social purpose.

Meanwhile, the trade press stood by holding up 10/10 scores in approval. None of them bothered to say that, when eventually the pool is drained, most will be seen to have been swimming naked.

No, instead the journos were busy ushering people up the ladder to the high board.

In September, *The Drum* announced its Social Purpose Awards aimed at celebrating "all organizations who are champions of change, and driving a more diverse, purposeful and socially responsible representation of marketing today."[6]

Which meant pretty much every creative agency in London.

Not to be outdone, *Campaign* spent the autumn organising its Purpose Summit.

Both were good indicators of the industry's priorities – and where the grubby business of helping clients turn a profit sat in the pecking order.

Indeed, on October 21st, I received this email promoting *Campaign's* event. It began:"Hi Stephen,There is no merit in profit without purpose. Recognising this, particularly in the wake of the coronavirus crisis, can be the key to your company's future success".[7]

Yes, that's what it said: "There is no merit in profit without purpose".

As I wrote on LinkedIn at the time,"Try explaining that

to those who see merit in employing staff, paying wages, keeping factories open, suppliers in business and paying taxes. And, as the Covid-19 recession bites, try running it past the poor bastards who wake at 4.00am worrying about laying off their staff, covering their debts, keeping their doors open and fending for their families."[8]

But that comment begged the question: could the person who wrote *Campaign's* email ever empathise with those "poor bastards"?

Not if they're a young warrior for social justice. In that case they'll probably see the capitalist business owner's sleep deprivation as just punishment for their exploitation of the workforce and despoiling of the environment.

Why creative work is easy with social purpose

Businesses small and large were crying out for advertising's profit-generating vaccine. But London's big agencies showed little interest in rolling it out.

Social purpose remained the priority. And why not?

For a culturally left-leaning industry, it allowed everyone to do the kind of work that pleased them personally. None of that dreadful, commercial selling stuff eh?

Better still, if they were bonused on awards won, then social purpose was the goose that kept producing the golden Lions.

And not only were they rewarded by their network bosses; they were also incentivised by their clients.

Justin Tindall was the ECD at Leo Burnett when he received the "Cannes Brief" from P&G's Marc Pritchard. It was sent to every agency on the P&G roster and, while social purpose-led, it had only one real purpose: winning an award.[9]

On pages 44-45 we saw how the judging was skewed towards this kind of work at Cannes in 2019.

The results of that showed up in WARC's ranking of the most awarded campaigns for 2020 at not just Cannes but such shows as D&AD, The One Show and the Clios.

Of the top 12, only six were aimed at persuading the prospect to actually buy a product or service. The other half were cause-related.[10]

No wonder.

If clients like P&G are out there Lion hunting, then in most networks there's a "Task Force" set up with the single minded objective of winning at Cannes.

And the task itself is simple. Find an issue that's trending and match that issue to an account held by the network.

As D&AD's Tim Lindsay conceded on page 171, it is possible to scam the system. And if you manage to "tick all the boxes" it can be easier to win a gong.[11]

Normally, award-winning work requires a big creative idea – the textbook definition of which is one that dramatises or demonstrates the benefit to the customer of the product being sold.

It's bloody difficult to do well. And often it is just as hard for the suits who have to sell that big creative idea to unimaginative or risk-averse clients, and their various stakeholders.

Most purpose-driven work avoids this painstaking act of bargaining and persuasion by taking the big idea out of the mix. For those executions, the creative idea lies simply in choosing the worthy cause. That's it. Then all you have to do is make a film about that cause and weave the brand in there.

How to win a Cannes Lion

Take, for instance, one of the big winners in WARC's list. Here's renowned planner Paul Feldwick's assessment: "The 2019 Cannes Gold Lion for 'brand experience and activation' went to Microsoft's X-Box for designing a console that could be used by the disabled. You might think that catering for disabled customers is something any brand today should be expected to do, but Microsoft obviously expected to get more credit for it, so they made a two minute TV commercial about it and put it on the Superbowl (estimated cost: $21m)."[12]

The only discernible idea here was to have disabled kids saying how much they enjoy gaming and how their X-Box console helps.

Loveable as they are, it's a series of talking heads.

Did a creative team get involved? Makes you wonder. Yet this film cleaned up at the big awards shows.

The lesson wasn't lost on youngsters coming into the industry.

And certainly not on those who entered Cream 2020, *Campaign* magazine's competition to discover the next breakthrough talent.

Of the 20 winning entries, only three were designed to get people to part with money. Only those three had a commercial purpose. In the other 17, there was no sales objective whatsoever. Again they were about social purpose. And, again, the big creative ideas were few and far between.[13]

Our own self-interest trumps social purpose

Speaking of young recruits, we're told by the advocates of social purpose that a business needs one if it is to attract the ethically-minded best and brightest.

But is that really the case? Let's look at our industry, should we?

In May 2021, Major Players published its research into what people look for in a job. Out of ten possible options, the top four were: "Work/Life Balance" 74%, "Interesting Work" 69%, "Culture" 65% and "Salary" 62%. Coming in tenth (behind "Benefits" on 29%) was "Purpose" on 20%.[14]

As the research into what motivates our purchase decisions that we saw on pages 155-156 indicated, in our industry self-interest trumps societal good every time.

But, sticking with the polls, what about those that show overwhelming public support for social purpose strategies?

It is true that many respondents will answer [X] when asked "Do you consider yourself a conscious consumer?" And [X] when asked "Would you boycott brands that exploit workers, refuse the right to unionise, pollute the environment and avoid paying their taxes?"

But having ticked those boxes, they'll likely pull out one of their several Apple devices and ping another order to Amazon (whose UK revenues rose by an astounding 51% in 2020).[15]

Why the disconnect?

Well, Director of Market Insight and Brand Strategy at Reach, Andrew Tenzer points out that such surveys usually rely on leading questions – like the two above.

He adds that, even when the questions are open, the desire to be seen as a "good" person leads respondents to tick the boxes that reflect well upon them.

In social science research this tendency to answer questions in a manner that will be viewed favourably by others is known as "social desirability bias". It can take the form of over-reporting "good behavior" or under-reporting "bad", or undesirable behavior. Either way, such answers can be discounted.

For good measure, Tenzer says, with characteristic bluntness, that "people are terrible at predicting their future behaviour."[16]

On the latter point Robin Brown VP, Insights & Advisory, Deloitte Canada added: "Consumers make choices that involve a wide range of influences. Many of them are unconscious. Singling out one potential influence and asking a direct question will overstate the importance of that influence."[17]

In other words, the pollsters' "ethical consumer" presents us with an over simplistic characterisation of human behaviour. We're best advised to remember the old research adage: "Ignore what people say: watch what they do".

Purpose works, doesn't it?

If you discount dodgy surveys from the argument for purpose, then what about the reports of greatly increased sales?

Just such a claim was made to me in October when I took part in a debate with Ayesha Walawalkar, Chief Strategy Officer at MullenLowe during the IPA's Effworks Week. In fighting her corner, Ayesha came up with the statistic that Omo/Persil's *Dirt is Good* campaign has resulted in a 10-fold increase in sales![18]

If that's the case then how wonderful. Ayesha, her colleagues and client have brought about the perfect marriage of social and commercial purpose.

Persil is one of the 28 brands that Unilever is promoting via its Sustainable Living Plan. In December, Alan Jope, the CEO, reported that these brands are growing twice as fast as others in the portfolio.[19]

That's impressive. But could it be there are other factors that explain the success of the purpose-driven brands? Like saliency and marketing spend? For example, we've all heard of Ben & Jerry's. But are you also familiar with these names: Telenti? Breyers? Grom? Darko? How about Klondike?

These are also Unilever ice cream brands. But they operate on the margins of Unilever's global marketing strategy. Meanwhile, Ben & Jerry's is highly successful because it is the focus of that marketing strategy.

It also has a long established reputation as a differentiated and excellent product. This is why the brand is famous. As *How Brands Grow* author, Byron Sharp, says:

"Ben & Jerry's is pointed out as one of the most purpose-driven brands. I would love to know how many consumers on the street have any idea about that. I think they would say:'That's the one with Cookie Dough isn't it?'"[20]

Consolidation in a crisis

No doubt Unilever's purpose-driven brands will have contributed even more to the overall profit of the company throughout 2020. And that's because the Covid-19 crisis has encouraged brand owners to cull the weaker local ones and consolidate spend round those with a global reach.

For example, Coke responded to plunging sales by weeding out "zombie brands", so-called because they offer little opportunity for growth and are often confined to a single country. This constituted 200 brands that made up just 2% of the company's revenue.[21]

Elsewhere, in July snack giant Mondelez announced plans for a 25% reduction in SKUs (stock-keeping units), which represented less than 2% of global sales. The idea was to simplify its supply chain while continuing to push ahead with innovation.[22]

Likewise, French food group Danone confirmed in November that it planned to reduce its range by 10%-30% in 2021, dropping small products that accounted for less than 2% of sales. The intention was to reinvest 20%-30% of savings into growth initiatives.[23]

It's worth sticking with Danone for a second to see how successful this paragon of social purpose has been.

Mmm? Danone

According to Valerie Hernando-Presse the Global CMO, brands can no longer be neutral, even in the face of controversy, and a clear political purpose is not only a good thing but an absolute necessity. She explains: "The way to thrive and survive is to have a reason why, beyond your product and profits, and to have a strong point of view on society. [Brands need] to take a stand on societal issues, to be ready to be divisive."

In light of the global catastrophe that's engulfed the world since February 2020, you might question whether brands should be adding to the collective anxiety and turmoil by being intentionally "divisive".

And you might add, "Who asked them to intervene in this way?"

But Ms Hernando-Presse swerves such issues and as the saviour of not just Danone but humankind she concludes: "Our main challenge is relevancy. If our brands are not bold enough, we will lose our meaning and, ultimately, we will die … It's about people. It's a shift from powerful people to people power."[24]

Her colleagues in the Danone's boardroom have, however, decided that it's actually about survival.

With sales dropping 1.5% in 2020 and Danone's share price at a seven year low, the group has made the "bold" move of trimming product ranges, selling off assets and cutting 2,000 jobs – including that of social purpose advocate Emmanuel Faber, the Chairman and CEO.[25]

If you were one of the other 2,000, then you might remind Ms Hernando-Presse that it is, indeed, about people. But it is also about profits – and if you're not making them then people suffer.

Plus ça change

Maybe Valerie Hernando-Presse was relying on a new kind of customer emerging from the Covid wreckage. One who'd be open to her kind of confrontational, conscientious marketing.

Others were betting on that, too. For example, the folks at KPMG.

As early as July 2020, they were saying: "Scratch the surface and the New Customer has profoundly changed; a generation of forced evolution has occurred in a handful of months. There has been a global psychological shift in values, beliefs and needs. Existing trends have been accelerated and new ones introduced. Customers feel more vulnerable, insecure and less in control than ever before. Values have evolved, with renewed demands that brands put integrity and purpose before profit."[26]

A first year student of Evolutionary Psychology would scoff at the idea of "a global psychological shift in values, beliefs and needs" within "a handful of months".

Likewise anyone who read December's Office for National Statistics report on the "new normal".

Apparently the New Customer lasted three months before the Old Customer showed up again.

"Evolved values"? Well, look, for example, at the increased burden of unpaid household labour and childcare that had fallen on wives and mothers.

Women had been penalised in the pandemic in other ways too. They were far more likely to have been furloughed, made redundant or forced to give up work when schools and nurseries shut.[27]

Old habits and roles hadn't evolved, they'd become entrenched.

That's what was happening in the real world anyway. But how about advertising's parallel universe?

15

2021
Delusion and reality

That ONS Survey came out at much the same time as *Campaign* was asking adland's luminaries for their thoughts on *The Year Ahead*.

Before we hear from them, it's worth pausing to recall just how terrible was the situation as Lockdown 3.0 bit.

The UK was "The Sick Man of Europe", recording 1,000 deaths every day throughout January.[1] Those millions who weren't lucky enough to be able to work from home were in mortal danger every time they went about their business.

Those who employed them were facing ruin.

The Institute for Public Policy Research said that almost 600,000 UK employers were at risk of business collapse in the spring if there is no extension of government coronavirus (COVID-19) support. Those employers accounted for a third of the UK's business turnover and employed around nine million people.

Carsten Jung, Senior Economist at the IPPR, said: 'This is a moment of great peril for more than half a million UK employers as their cash reserves run perilously low and their businesses hang on by a thread."[2]

Rishi Sunak spoke of "the scarring" of the economy, but in some parts of the country it was being eviscerated. You could see the open wounds not just in the 813,000 people who'd lost their jobs in 2020 but in the soaring rates of suicide and shoplifting amongst our fellow citizens.[3]

By far the worst hit were the disadvantaged people who adland's social justice warriors spent much of their time talking about.

Yet, judging by the thoughts they shared with

Campaign, our industry leaders were totally oblivious to this crisis and the unique role advertising could play in bringing jobs, wages, growth and social healing.

With the exception (again) of Nigel Vaz, not one of the 24 contributors spoke about the issue that was keeping the rest of the country awake at night – and what the ad industry might do to help.[4]

One reason why no one else referenced either was hinted at by James Murphy. In his piece he said the ad industry seemed "afraid of its own shadow and ashamed of its core purpose."[5]

Predictably some fell back on social purpose and took turns to talk about "walking in step with the need to face our ethical issues" and to tell us that "brands that have a clear and ethical purpose and do the right thing will win" and "a brand's credibility will be measured by their ethical contributions."[6]

Little if any reference was made to advertising's role in financing these "ethical contributions". Indeed, generating the profit that would pay for them and other things like wage bills, taxes, capital investment and R&D funding were not discussed.

It was all whimsically detached from any concrete reality, and put me in mind of something that Benjamin Braun, Samsung's CMO Europe, had written in *The Drum* a couple of months earlier.

Braun, who'd presided over the commercially successful *Compare the Meerkat* and *Audi/Clowns* campaigns, was noting the consequences of adland's disregard for effectiveness and evidence-based thinking: "Now, chief finance officers and chief executives have no interest in joining the meeting when a creative agency comes knocking — by and large, it'll be the chief marketing officer who handles it. But trust me, when someone like McKinsey is at the door of a company to talk about marketing, it's not the CMO who opens it."[7]

The empathisers' new clothes

Was it an attempt to cling to some kind of relevance? Or was it their sense of entitlement? Either way, as the doors slammed, and the power and influence of the creative agencies waned, they became ever more eager to tell everyone else what to do.

The general assumption, sorry, *insistence* was that the commitment to social purpose and its concomitant progressive politics be shared by everyone. Take, for example, the piece written by Lucy Jameson, the founder of Uncommon Creative Studios.

She got off to a great start by advocating "empathy. Fierce, uncompromising empathy." It got better as she talked of the need to "break out of our social media and support bubbles" to "walk the unfamiliar streets, to visit other peoples shops, to have a chat and a rummage round their houses".

Let's assume she was talking about ordinary people here.

But when it was all going so well, she concluded that "understanding alone is not enough". We need to be like those poster girls of the Liberal left, Megan Rapinhoe and Kamala Harris. And make sure that "ferocious caring needs to come to the fore" as we "pave the way to a different reaction."[8]

In other words, we need to find out what the culturally conservative mainstream think and feel. We need to learn how, as we saw on pages 28-30, their morality has different foundations. And we need to understand the Binding ethics that inform their lives.

And then, with renewed zeal, we should set about promoting our purpose-driven agenda to them – whether they want it or not.

Like Kipling's (can I still even mention him?) *Gods of the Copybook Headings*, the finding of Tenzer and Murray's *Empathy Delusion* keep returning to mock us.

Lucy Jameson did at least acknowledge the need to reconnect with our audience. Other contributors seemed intent on showing how caught up they were in their own world.

Here's Emma Chiu, the Global Director at Wunderman Thompson Intelligence: "Expect to see more career opportunities that better facilitate remote work environments … After all, why work from home when you can work from Barbados?"[9] Why indeed, Emma?

At least I understood that. But I'm still trying to get my head round this from Jonathan Emmins, the founder of Amplify: "We are now in an era of nomadic experiences with a flex on experience output versus scale. But hyper-local and scale don't need to be mutually exclusive. Audiences now embrace kinship as a shared sense of place, identity, practice and role in society – wherever they are in the world."[10]

Barbados, perhaps?

Why didn't we want to help?

Remember back in April 2020 (and page 126) when Craig Mawdsley called Covid-19 "the biggest event since the Second World War"? Well, clearly from *Campaign's The Year Ahead*, it was a fight that no one in adland wanted any part of.

How do we explain this declaration of neutrality in the war everyone else in Britain was waging?

They could have been a force for good. But the way in which that "good" would have been achieved suited neither their self-image or their politics. Which, in the case of left-leaning progressives, is often one and the same thing.

Time and again, throughout this book, we've noted how uncomfortable they are with advertising's commercial purpose. We've also seen how detached they are from the rest of the population.

Distance has not lent enchantment. The opposite, in fact.

Not only do they feel separate. On occasion, they're hostile. Here's a microaggression for you: on February 3rd, one of the industry's most respected strategists, Robert Campbell tweeted:

"I am beside myself with happiness. Today I got one of my clients to sign off on an creative criteria that states: 'if our work does not ignite publishable anger among *Daily Mail* editorial staff, we have not pushed hard enough'."[11]

As we know the *Daily Mail* is shorthand for middle England and a political/cultural perspective shared by millions of voters. In progressive left circles, it often prompts derogatory references to "Gammons" and "Karens".

Anyway, 179 people liked Robert's comment, the consensus being "this is the dream brief", and that antagonising the mainstream is a hoot.

In mitigation, it could be that Robert's client has an overtly left-leaning target audience and that a partisan positioning will appeal to them. In which case, the objective was valid.

But then again … on March 3rd he departed these shores for a job in New Zealand tweeting: "Thank you England. You were very special. See you again. Oh, and fuck you Tory scum".[12]

So no, I think it's safe to say that Robert is full of scorn. Which isn't great at the best of times. And especially not when a part of your job is writing strategies that are aimed at the very people you scorn the most.

The Revolt of the Elites

Interestingly, Robert Campbell's partner at the School of Strategic Arts, Martin Weigel has warned "As for creatives who believe real people in the real world are morons whose opinions they can and should ignore, they might want to contemplate whether they should find another profession. It's hard to do great work for people you despise."[13]

But despise them, we do.

As I pointed out on page 96, when the cultural elites

talk about the mainstream, it's with a mixture of condescension and contempt. Of course, this antipathy is, nothing new. The upper classes have always looked down their noses at the *hoi polloi*.

But we, in advertising, are part of a new elite that was first identified in the mid-1990s by the left-leaning social critic and historian, Christopher Lasch. As he had it, "they control the international flow of money and information, preside over philanthropic foundations and institutions of higher learning, manage the instruments of cultural production, and thus set the terms of public debate." [14]

It is, however, a debate that, for example, the readers of the *Daily Mail*, are not encouraged to join. As Lasch had it: "Simultaneously arrogant and insecure, the new elites regard the masses with mingled scorn and apprehension." [15]

Earlier we saw how Lasch's observations have been updated by the likes of David Goodhart (*The Road to Somewhere*) and Elizabeth Currid-Halkett (*The Sum of Small Things*).

Deborah Mattinson (*Beyond the Red Wall*) gives us the view from the other direction – with the masses' sense of being "overlooked, sneered at and looked down upon." [16]

All three writers explain how a culturally left-leaning, university-educated, metropolitan, clerisy have severed their connection with the people beyond their bubble.

According to American academic Matthew B Crawford, "Instead of feeling bound up in a shared fate with one's countrymen, one develops an alternate solidarity that is placeless." [17]

And it is precisely this that we saw in adland's

indifference to the pandemic/economic crisis that was gripping the country, and our refusal to even discuss ways we might ameliorate its impact.

Back to reality

Many of the contributors to *Campaign's The Year Ahead* had their heads in much the same place as Andy Bunday described on page 164

But when forced to remove them and look at the numbers, they had to admit the picture was grim.

In January, *Campaign* asked the industry what the year looked like financially and, while media and digital all saw grounds for some optimism in 2021, the creative shops couldn't see beyond the gloom.[18]

The situation was worst amongst those owned by the big holding companies. And it wasn't simply because of the Covid crisis. Problems here were deep-seated.

Take WPP, for example. In its Capital Markets Day, it revealed that from 2014-19, all its creative agencies suffered negative net sales growth (revenue less pass-through costs) – a marked contrast from their media and digital counterparts.[19]

Campaign jumped on this on February 8th, asking *Are creative shops on borrowed time?*

The evidence was provided by Moore Kingston Smith's annual survey of agency performance which revealed that the 20 agencies owned by listed groups showed a collective compound annual growth rate of just 1%, with half showing a decline.

The 15 independents were not much better. For them the figure was 6% with a third showing decline.[20]

When asked what the solution might be, no one came out and said the obvious thing – start proving your value to your clients by building their brands and selling their products on the strength of how useful they might be to the customer. And start doing it not just in 30 second spots but at all those moments of truth (remember them?) when the prospect encounters either the thing being sold or their possible need for it.

As usual, James Murphy delivered one of his bulletins from the world of commercial reality: "There isn't a shortage of opportunities for creative agencies to grow. But there's a shortage of the talent that can convert those opportunities into growth."[21]

Time, however, was running out.

Over at Dentsu, the 2020 media mix had been 47% media, 30% CXM and 23% creative. In terms of performance, CXM was down only 3.2% (and Merkle just 1.3%) while media dropped 15.6% and creative plunged 18%.

By February 2021 CEO Wendy Clark had seen enough and announced that by 2025 customer experience capabilities would represent half of revenue. No prizes for guessing at whose expense.[22]

16
New blood
New hope

The writing on the wall was as clear to see as a back-lit, 96 sheet special build. And Wendy Clark wasn't the only one to notice.

Some recognised the flaws in the places they worked and felt they could do better. Others saw the ever diminishing opportunities that lay before them if they stayed put. Others were just sick of the politics.

Whatever the reason, in the 12 months after Covid-19 began there were more start-ups than had emerged in the previous five years.

In October alone, there were six high-profile agency launches. These included Mother's spin-off shop Other, ScienceMagic, Friendly Giants, and Platform

There was also The Constellation Collective set up by Former Grey London Creative Chairman Adrian Rossi, ex-Domino's Chief Marketer Emily Somers and founder Simon Thurston; while former MullenLowe Open executives Ant Hopper and Si Goodall launched a customer experience consultancy The Ninety-Niners.

Other new ventures were zooming in on potential clients. There was creative shop Motel, founded by Rob Smith, the former Chief Client Officer at McCann Worldgroup, and Lee Tan, the multi award-winning ECD at the same agency; and the colourfully named Orange Panther Collective, founded by four former London agency pros.

Alex Buxton, the IPA's Head of New Business, who oversees its Accelerator programme for up-and-coming agencies, said he'd seen "a huge amount" of start-ups across the industry."[1]

There have also been a spate of consultancies set up by

high profile planners. Perhaps the most illustrious being that of former AMV/BBDO strategist Craig Mawdsley and Bridget Angear. Another is The Barber Shop led by Dino Myers-Lamptey (ex-MullenLowe Mediahub),

Myers-Lamptey revealed that planning has become "very unfulfilling" at big agencies because people attach themselves to "meaty" global accounts to justify their positions. But working on such accounts is not enjoyable because people "can't necessarily see the impact of their work that quickly".[2]

Another former network employee turned start-up entrepreneur put it more bluntly. He told me that on those global accounts the "work is just part of the tool kit of retention. Efficacy isn't a determinant of success. Just getting to the other side of the black hole with the client still on board is the aim".

In other words, they don't have a clue whether they've sold anything or not.

Nor whether they've been talking to the customers in a way those people will understand.

Talking to real customers

That's not a mistake that former MullenLowe Open executives, Ant Hopper and Si Goodall, will make. They have called their consultancy "The Ninety-Niners" to convey how the business will "stand with the 99%; the real customers who experience brands, not the 1% who create them".[3]

And they are revelling in the opportunity to have that

direct consumer contact – and "do the job we love again, adding value to the client's business".

It's worth noting that Hopper and Goodall originated one of the most commercially effective and socially beneficial campaigns ever devised – and they did so long before the social purpose bandwagon rumbled over the horizon.

It's 15 years since they led the launch of the *1 Pack – 1 Vaccine* initiative for P&G's Pampers. Whilst selling tens of million of packets of diapers, an estimated 750,000 newborn lives have been saved and 150 million women and their newborns protected from the deadly disease, maternal and newborn tetanus.

Goodall, however, is clear about the priorities of those who made it.

"We started with the existing brand purpose of 'caring for baby's development' and knew that new mums are highly empathetic towards other babies. But our aim, first and foremost, was to sell product. The *1 Pack – 1 Vaccine* mechanic is designed to add tangible value to every single pack of nappies and help Pampers negotiate more merchandising space with retail customers like Tesco and Asda. It has been running for so long not because of the lives saved, but because it serves Pampers' commercial purpose."

It seems he'll be adopting the same approach for clients at his new consultancy: "Social purpose is the wrong starting point. We are more interested in the customer's purpose. Rather than beginning with the dubious question 'why do we exist in the world, beyond making money', brands should start by asking 'why do we

exist for our consumers, beyond our functional benefit?'
Sometimes those things will overlap, but mostly they
won't."[4]

"We're here to sell stuff"

I know, from my own experience of setting up shop, that
little brings out the inner salesperson like waiting around
for the phone to ring.

When that call comes, the tendency is to talk up the
tangible difference you can make to the prospective
client on the other end of the phone.

I imagine things won't have changed since my day. And
the entrepreneurs running the new agencies and consultancies are quickly re-discovering their commercial
purpose.

Rob Smith, the founder of Motel told me "We talk about
how to make your budget work harder, not always about
sales. But then again, I wonder if we're just a little too polite
to say that."[5] Rob's partner, Lee Tan, has no such qualms:
"We're here to solve client problems and, yes, sell stuff."[6]

The emphasis is on effectiveness, and why these new
shops are different enough – and talented enough – to
achieve it.

As Simon Thurston who leads the Constellation
Collective told me, "Our core proposition is generating
growth. We are at the cutting edge of commercial survival
and if we aren't talking to our clients about progressing
their prospects down the brand/sales funnel then we
won't be here in six months' time."[7]

It's likely there'll be a receptive audience for such a back-to-basics message. Especially as the start-ups will probably be too small or too new to get any RFPs from those multinationals who are less concerned about the sales from their last campaign.

The clients that gravitate to the new shops will be more business-like and results oriented.

Which means they'll be interested in innovative, effective ideas rather than formulaic tropes aimed at winning awards.

The work they buy will reflect that. And that can only be good for the industry.

The commercial equivalent of B Corp certification

The same can be said of the new President of the IPA, Julian Douglas.

On March 25th he used his inaugural address to outline the organisation's commitment to measurable brand building and sales.

The flagship initiative is the IPA Effectiveness Accreditation programme, a scheme for member agencies aimed at "creating processes, environments, attitudes and, ultimately, values that deliver pride in the business results of what we do for our clients and ourselves." As Douglas said, this is an effort to create an "effectiveness culture within agencies day-to-day".[8]

Agencies were asked to submit a paper and video by May 26th, 2021. Successful entrants will receive their accreditation by September 2021. They will then be reviewed on a rolling two year basis.

According to the IPA, this "will help agencies to position themselves as true business growth partners to brands ... create a measure of distinction between agencies ... help the industry to create a culture in which effectiveness is not only a goal, but, in time, a basic requirement, an expectation between brand marketers and agencies ... and help clients to justify and validate their choice of agency and the work they produce for them."[9]

It looks very much like this will be to commercial purpose what B Corp is to social purpose. And, one hopes, will be treated with the same respect and recognition.

Sharpening the industry's business edge

Douglas didn't stop there. In the drive to sharpen the industry's commercial edge he announced plans to increase the number of executives completing the IPA's MBA Essentials qualification, run in partnership with the London School of Economics.

Moreover, there'll be a series of partnerships with the "very best" companies working in gaming around the world. It's hoped that exposure to the technical and commercial brilliance of companies like Epic Games might rub off.

As Douglas said, "This sector is bigger than the movie and music industry combined, and with the explosion of mobile gaming, is growing at pace ... Yet it is still largely overlooked by us as an industry." [10]

In other words: Wake up! This is what creativity actually looks like and can achieve in the 2020s.

That thought also lies behind the IPA's plans to forge a new partnership with Facebook. The aim is to develop Augmented Reality in marketing through educational seminars and practical workshops.

There's also plenty of business nous behind Douglas's call on IPA members to accompany him on a trade mission to India "to meet, learn from and collaborate with new tech partners in the world's biggest democracy and emergent economy – Asia's answer, and increasingly rival, to Silicon Valley". [11]

Making the Effectiveness Awards more effective

It's all very encouraging. But there's one extra, simple tweak that Julian Douglas can make that will further inculcate the results-based culture.

At the moment the IPA Effectiveness Awards are run once every two years. Why? If the aim is to refocus the industry on work that works and the thinking behind it then it would be more, yes, effective to do this on an annual basis.

That way, campaigns that are still top-of-mind in the industry can be lionised. And, quite simply, the more good examples of best practice we get, the better.

There were plenty of good examples in the most recent awards announced in October, 2020.

Six were given to not-for-profit organisations. Otherwise, of the 19 other Gold, Silver and Bronze winners, only one had an element of social purpose in their strategy.[12]

The successful submissions by Tesco, Audi, Diageo, Guinness, John Lewis, Baileys et al were built upon a benefit aimed specifically at the target consumer and not around an intention to solve society's problems.

And that success wasn't recorded in link clicks, shares, messaging connections, video views or a film showing very quick cuts of favourable responses posted on social media.

It was measured in profit generated for every pound invested.

Unlocking adland's gated community

From Julian Douglas's inaugural speech, it's clear the new President of the IPA has no problems with advertising's commercial purpose.

A proud Mancunian with a Jamaican father and an Irish mum, you sense he's also the man to lead working class talent into adland's middle class gated community.

As the Chair of the Talent Group (2016-2020), he helped launch Advertising Unlocked back in 2017 aimed at introducing school kids from all backgrounds to the industry. He was also instrumental in creating the iList of individuals who are actively making the industry more open to people other than the university-educated elites.

In fairness, those elites do appear to be making some room for outsiders.

Ogilvy got started long before the pressure from the BLM protests spurred the industry into action. Its apprentice scheme, The Pipe, began back in 2016 and many of its alumni are now working in the agency.

According to *The Guardian* "the scheme has seen Ogilvy welcome poets, skaters, sculptors, jewellery designers, shelf stackers, artists and DJs through its doors."[13] Shelf stackers aside, I'm not sure that too many of them will provide the agency with the working class worldview it badly needs. But I suppose they're trying.

Most of the other holding companies are following suit with their own apprenticeship programmes for those from disadvantaged and minority backgrounds.

This February, Publicis Groupe launched The Open Apprenticeship, an interactive platform offering an entry point for people who want to grasp the basics of the industry, types of jobs on offer and the careers they might lead to.

It's an ambitious project, aiming to reach 10,000 people in its first year and then guiding some of them towards jobs within the network

Dear old London

A few will be heading to Saatchi & Saatchi who are offering rent-free/heavily subsidised accommodation for interns who live outside of London; subsidised accommodation for Saatchi Open candidates; and preferential rates for all junior agency talent below a set salary threshold.

The cost of living in London has become an increasingly high barrier to working class youngsters who want a start in the industry. So initiatives like this can only help.

But will they be enough?

Those who live in the capital will still get most of the jobs. Their close proximity to the agencies means they can live at home while they find their feet.

But there's more to it than that. A disadvantaged youngster in London is almost twice as likely to enter university as one from the regions.[14] So they'll have the academic qualifications that adland fixates on. Whereas youngsters from outside London won't make it into the next "grads intake".

This London-centric aspect of the industry is a huge problem.

Nearly 32,000 people work for the big six global agency groups in the UK (even after Covid-19 job cuts) and about 27,000, or around 85%, work in London.

Geographical bias is greater among the three largest groups: 90% of WPP's 10,000 staff and Omnicom's 6,500 people and 95% of Publicis Groupe's 5,000 employees work in London.[15]

Any efforts to break down the domination of advertising's metropolitan Anywheres can only be a good thing for the industry.

The encouraging news is, many talented youngsters have given up on London and are now looking to the regions' Somewhere agencies I mentioned earlier.

The capital's lost its allure

Dave Warfield, Creative Lead at Cardiff's S3 Advertising, told me that when he was a student at Falmouth he was shocked by the attitude of the ECDs who visited from the larger agencies: "It was all ego and 'The Big I Am'. Rather than coming to inspire us, they were very arrogant and we were insignificant in their eyes. It put a lot of us off straight away".

That initial doubt was reinforced by the time spent in London on placement. "The excitement and the dream met with reality very quickly. Unless you've got rich parents or saved up a lot yourself, you can't afford to stay in London after the placement looking for a job."

Dave has also found you get a lot more respect, responsibility and opportunity to learn your craft in a regional agency. And he's not alone in his choice. He says that, of the 30 teams who were on his course, only four have gone to London. Indeed, students at Falmouth are now encouraged by their course leader "to put regional agencies on a par with those in London".[16]

London's lost allure was also commented upon by Kevin Darton, Lecturer in Creative Advertising at University of Central Lancashire. His students have the Somewhere's mistrust and even disdain for the capital. They also have a level-headed approach to their politics: "They're almost all northern working class students and they see right through brand purpose stuff before they even get to me. They're totally on board when it's done appropriately but have no time for those who jump on the bandwagon."[17]

Michael Hayes, copywriter and planner at Leeds's HOME agency put it more bluntly: "Who wants to work six days a week, for average pay, in one of the most expensive cities in the world? While listening to people talk shit about a culture war they expect you to join?"[18]

The place he works is one of the most successful in the UK, with billings in 2019 that pushed it into the top 25 UK agencies.

His boss Richard Dudleston says: "We aren't seeking a purpose any more honourable than doing what we're paid for – keeping a clear focus on our clients' business and their commercial success. And, indirectly of course, our own success and the appropriate reward and fulfilment of our people "

He also has an interesting insight into why regional agencies, like his, have remained so pragmatic. He reckons that people who work in media necessarily have a more business-like and data-driven understanding of the audience that ads are aimed at. As such they are a grounding influence on the people around them.

But when London's media and creative shops separated well over a decade ago, the latter escaped their orbit and drifted from the transactional to the transcendental.[19]

Levelling up

Other people I spoke to cited more basic influences.

Gary McNulty is now a Creative Director as Manchester's 450 strong Havas Lynx. A Mancunian himself, he says "Being back here, you chat to your neighbours, you hear people on the bus, and then you think about, say Maltesers and how they're going to help with postnatal depression. And you know these people see the bullshit in campaigns like that."[20]

Gary came back to Manchester after successful stints at shops like BBH and Grey (when they were great). He's not alone in making that trip.

Andy Bunday, Creative Director at The&Partnership in Manchester, is another returnee having worked at HHCL and RKCR/YR. He says, "The direction of travel is more out of London than at any time in the past 30 years. It used to be a one-way street heading south but now it is easier than ever to hire junior and middleweight people. And the more senior ones, the leaders, are thinking they've had enough of London and they're coming back home."[21]

Some are doing so because their network bosses have realised they need a presence in the regions.

WPP is building its Manchester Campus bringing MediaCom, Wavemaker, Code Computer Love, Kinetic and Cheetham Bell under one roof.

They're following in the wake of Dentsu. Close to 2,700 staff are still in London, but upwards of 500 staff work in Manchester and 350 in Edinburgh, plus the group has offices in other cities including Bristol, Derby, Leeds and Newcastle.

Oliver has joined the exodus and is opening an office in Cardiff. However, it has already escaped the London bubble through its specialisation in in-housing.

The agency works with clients throughout the UK and sources its own staff from local talent. As Chris

Woodward, the CEO told me this means "the composition of our people is much more representative of the country as a whole." Chris echoes Richard Dudleston when he says the focus is on "keeping the client's commercial engines running." And perhaps this, and the diverse profile of its staff, is why Oliver saw growth of 37% last year at a time when most London-based agencies suffered losses of between -20 and -50%.[22]

As I write, I hear that Deloitte is opening in Leeds and Ogilvy in Manchester. And you can expect more moves into the regions as business responds to the government's levelling up initiatives.

For example, Goldman Sachs has just announced its decision to open new offices in Birmingham where it will be joining the likes of HSBC, PwC and Deutsche Bank who've already set up bases in the West Midlands.

Cash-strapped London agencies will doubtless follow the money, quite literally in this case. And hopefully when that money talks, it will do so with a down-to-earth regional accent.

But still they keep walloping on the woke wash

Encouraging as these signs are, adland is still walloping the woke wash all over its briefs.

Everyone's favourite advertiser, Burger King, was caught brush in hand on two occasions in March.

First, Global CMO Fer Machado sent out news that Burger King "once again steps up to help people and communities". The brand was bailing out France's beleaguered farmers by buying up 200 tonnes of potatoes and giving them away at their restaurants in one kilo bags.

The post came complete with a shot of the spuds' packaging which had the headline: "We're keeping French farmers feeling chipper" along with some nicely written copy beneath.[23]

Why the English version, with the deft play on words? Because that's the language of the international advertising awards juries – and they were the key audience for this publicity stunt.

Too harsh?

OK, how about this: in 2020 French farmers produced 6,758,800 tonnes of spuds. So BK relieved those fermiers of 0.002% of the crop – or the output of a 10 hectare farm. In other words, small potatoes.[24]

A couple of weeks later BK was at it again. This time they were exploiting International Women's Day by pointing out how too few women occupy jobs of status in the restaurant world's kitchens. And how BK were correcting this by offering two $25,000 grants to females wanting to further their culinary education.

They got into big trouble by promoting this with the sexist headline: "Women belong in the kitchen".

And then some people also worked out that Burger King had spent in excess of $210,000 on a full page advertising their largesse. So, $50,000 to solve the problem versus over four times that much to draw attention to BK's caring, kind, socially progressive gesture.[25]

If you want examples of what's wrong with this social purpose racket, there's two whoppers for you.

Thankfully, Machado's counterpart at Yum! Brands (KFC and Pizza Hut), Ken Muench, has a more, dare we say, honest approach. He is all for companies acting responsibly and can point to the $100m that his organisation has invested to fight inequality across the company and communities.

But he is adamant that CSR does not translate into marketing strategy. As he said a few weeks after Machado's shenanigans: "[Brand purpose] truly is a bunch of crap, because it's disingenuous. You're saying, 'My purpose is to make the world a better place'. No, your purpose is to make money."[26]

The truth is, Machado believes this, too. He recently tweeted: "I find it funny when people react to an idea we did by saying 'but did it sell?' The answer usually is 'yes' . . . Our largest shareholder is a private equity company. 'Sell or else'. (That's a phrase from David Ogilvy)".[27]

So Muench and Machado agree about their commercial purpose. It's just that, on the evidence of the above examples, one of them is a little less scrupulous about achieving it.

Campaign finally responds

When adland's favourite CMO is signing off scams, you know things aren't right.

And you'd like to think that our trade press would see through them, and was objective and sceptical enough to keep the industry honest.

In the past, *Campaign* would run its "Turkey of the

Week" which held to account the client and agency who'd produced the biggest creative travesty of the past seven days.

Now there's a greater need for "Woke Wash of the Week".

But would *Campaign* do it? Well until recently I'd have said "No". It is one of the industry institutions that ardently promotes social purpose and is the mouthpiece for progessive ideas.

And yet – and here's another reason to be hopeful – in March the trade paper finally responded to my request to air my argument in its pages.

It had taken quite some time, believe me.

Back in December 2019 I'd written to the then Executive Editor, Claire Beale, with a pdf of the original draft of *Can't Sell, Won't Sell* and a request for observations. I then sent her two follow-up emails.

No reply.

When the book came out in August, I wrote to her successor, Gideon Spanier, twice with much the same request.

And I got much the same response.

I then tried one of the magazine's most senior journalists, Jeremy Lee. Nothing came of that.

Remember, this is a book recommended by, amongst many others, Jeremy Bullmore, Paul Burke, Dave Trott, Dave Dye, Mark Ritson, Marc Lewis, Vikki Ross, Richard Huntington and George Tannenbaum.

Finally, in December, Maisie McCabe, the UK Editor, got in touch and asked me for an article. Her plan was to run it alongside an interview with Paul Feldwick and bill it as "A Provocation".

Paul's premise was that the industry is cut off from the mainstream and has lost the ability to entertain and engage with its audience.[28]

Mine, as you can imagine, was about the need for advertising to reboot its commercial purpose in order to help the country through the post-pandemic recession.[29]

Paul and I were merely reminding the industry of its fundamental roles. For this to be billed as "Provocation" tells you much about *Campaign's* editorial position and the points of view it usually presses on its readers.

The fact that *Campaign* was surprised by the lack of negative feedback showed, once again, how largely unrepresentative those points of view happen to be.

How did our institutions let this happen?

I hoped this response might encourage *Campaign* – one of adland's key institutions – to be more open to arguments that run counter to the industry groupthink.

As we've seen, with the exception of the IPA, those institutions have failed to make the case for advertising's commercial purpose and its positive role in a free market economy and UK society.

Perhaps more damningly, they've neglected to emphasise the contribution that good advertising makes to a client's bottom line.

The result? Well, on May 12th, one industry leader took to LinkedIn to complain that clients no longer appreciate the time and talent required to produce a quality product. Nor do they realise that this costs money. They want it quick and cheap. So "where once the public rather liked advertising and we liked working in the business, our consuming public now do pretty much anything to avoid it, and sadly a lot of us are looking for ways to leave."[30]

The author of this bleak vision? Tim Lindsay, the Chairman of D&AD.

A day later, he took to *Campaign* to again blame clients who refused to pay their agencies enough money. He then lamented "What was once a powerful business tool, that was capable of inserting itself into popular culture, that people said they liked as much or more than the programmes is debased and devalued."[31]

On LinkedIn, he'd closed by asking "How have we let this happen?" as if his organisation had no responsibility for what he implied is the inexorable decline of a once brilliantly creative industry.

The truth is that this "powerful business tool" has been "debased and devalued" while Tim has been running one of the world's most influential advertising bodies.

In light of what he wrote, convincing clients of the commercial value added by excellent, effective creative work should surely have been the top priority of D&AD. Likewise WACL, the Advertising Association, *Campaign, Creative Review, The Drum*, the DMA etc. And, given its fundamental importance to the industry's survival, this message should now be their equivalent of Cato the Elder's "*Carthago delenda est*".

Unfortunately instead of lobbying, they've been preaching. Rather than saving our industry, they've been more intent on saving the world – and in promoting advertising that sells a progressive agenda that a conservative "consuming public now do pretty much anything to avoid".

What's the point of advertising?

Our institutions should be making the case for work that works. And not only to clients but also to people in the industry.

Since writing this book, I've met young recruits who've told me they'd never realised that selling and generating a profit might have a beneficial impact.

But it gets worse. Last week, I was asked by a very bright student if I'd critique his book. Like so many others, it was full of ads about LGBT rights, transexuality and post-colonial guilt. In short, the kind of gesture politics that would prove wholly ineffectual if force-fed to the mainstream. And probably pretty irritating.

It's not the youngster's fault. Just look at the laughably predictable winners of the Black Pencils at the latest D&AD awards. The student was simply reflecting our institutions' relentless focus on social issues.

If, at the moment, they were asked the question: "What is the point of advertising?" selling wouldn't get a mention. As James Murphy has pointed out more than once, the ad industry is ashamed to talk about its fundamental purpose.[32]

Sir John Hegarty noted this when, on March 24th, he observed, "the creative world has withdrawn almost from representing true commercial issues, as in: 'I'm selling a product here, these are the values that surround this product, and this is why you should buy it.' We've almost withdrawn from that and I think it's a great shame."[33]

Instead, our institutions are fixated with societal change and have fallen for the fiction that a small group of agitators and careerists represent the conscience – and future – of the industry. (Many of whom have found a safe haven within those institutions.)

To help rid adland of the shame to which both Sir John and James Murphy refer, and to reconnect with both clients and mainstream, our institutions should follow the advice of Culture Secretary, Oliver Dowden. He wants people from the Midlands and the North to join management of top cultural organisations and give them "the courage to stand up against the political fads and noisy movements of the moment."[34]

Justine Wright or Andy Bunday for President of D&AD, perhaps. Or maybe a role at the Advertising Association.

As we noted on pages 130 and 131, the Advertising Association paid scant attention to Covid-19's impact on the economy and the industry. Nothing has changed. In March they asked me to take part in a debate during which the AA were intending to support the motion that every ad should be green "in the message that it carries".[35]

The fact the people at the AA even considered this indicates the extremity of their views. And while most people in advertising are sympathetic to environmental causes, they do not subscribe to this radical groupthink. Yet they do not have a conduit for their opinions. Indeed, many are reluctant and even afraid to speak out.

"Abject fear"

Several of the interviewees for this book asked to remain anonymous. One even took the precaution of not using the agency email for fear their views could be read by others – and held against them. Another told me "there's an absolute abject fear of putting your head above the parapet." A blogger who's otherwise famous for their fearlessly controversial views pleaded the Fifth when asked to comment.

And this used to be an industry for mavericks.

In chapter 10, I noted the coddling of adland's mind and the suffocating monoculture it helped sustain. Our trade papers, industry bodies and the heads of agencies and holding companies need to acknowledge and challenge this. If they're serious about diversity, they should foster an environment of intellectual openness and freedom of thought.

For example, it should be permissible for someone to paraphrase Dr Martin Luther King Jr. and say; "a creative team should not be judged by the colour of their skin, class or gender, but by the quality of their book." I imagine most people in our industry could see the validity in that view. But, right now, to openly endorse it could get them fired.

Our institutions need to protect that right, reflect all opinions and serve the needs of the 190,000 people who work in the advertising and marketing sub-sector of the UK's creative industries. Especially those outside the M25, who constitute over half that number.

By embracing such a diverse audience and being more inclusive, they might get to the cause of the tension and fear I alluded to on page 176. And play a vital part in dispelling it.

Why ESG and CSR are important ...

As I said, *Campaign's* gesture was a small step in the right direction. In my case, it allowed me to make some fundamental points to the audience I most wanted to address.

I say fundamental, and for the sake of clarification – and the good of the industry – they are worth making once again.

The first is that clients should be encouraged to pursue ESG or CSR as corporate strategy.

As Paul Feldwick explained:"Any company's 'corporate social responsibility' begins with 1) Pay your taxes. 2) Treat your employees well. 3) Treat your suppliers well. 4) Treat your customers well. 5) Respect the environment. If you still have more profits than you think you need, invest them in points 2-5. If you're reduced to philanthropy, don't parade it as a virtue."[36]

At the moment advertising agencies spend too much time parading their own and their clients' virtues. They should remember that their primary purpose is to generate the sales that enable their clients to fund points 1-5.

Secondly, marketing strategies that solve society's problems can be commercially very effective. In the previous pages I've cited the likes of REI, BT, Persil and Pampers.

If you want further evidence see Thomas Kolster's new 42courses sessions on *Goodvertising*.[37] Or look at the success of, say, Brewdog – er, actually, perhaps not.[38] Think instead of Doisy & Dam (while munching their Dark Chocolate Truffles).

So, it's not either/or when it comes to social and commercial purpose.

But we should use social purpose judiciously, asking: "Will it help achieve my client's fundamental need: demand generation?"

... but why commercial purpose takes precedence

If we doubt the importance of this, our commercial purpose, we should remind ourselves that every time someone buys something we've advertised, we enable someone else to get paid. And not just the person in the shop where it was purchased. That sale pays the wages of the person who made the thing. Or grew it. The person who packaged it. The person in the warehouse where it was stored. The person who delivered it to the shop. And the person who cleaned the shop after closing time.

We must also realise that if there's no sale, there's no profit. And without profit then our clients' commitment to CSR or ESG will, despite everyone's laudable intentions, ebb away.

Moreover, if we fail to make the case for the full-funnel, brand-building, sales-driving work that will stoke sustained growth, then client-side CEOs will continue to divert budgets to the direct and digital sales activation shops.

Indeed if we do not make this our go-to-market proposition, then those CEOs will wonder if they can trust us with anything. And, as Benjamin Braun warned, pick up the phone to Accenture, Deloitte or S4 Capital.

Which means once-proud agencies like M&C Saatchi, Grey London, Wieden + Kennedy, Wunderman Thompson and AMV, will struggle to recover from a year when billings shrank -46.2%, -44.3% -40.3% -32.9% and -31.2% respectively.[39]

And what will be left?

Well, we'll continue congratulating ourselves on our ability to work remotely (oblivious to how privileged we are to be able do so), condemning ourselves for our lack of ethnic and gender diversity (while ignoring the class, age, disability or cognitive varieties) and consoling ourselves with our Yellow Pencils (for work that may never have run).

In short, while competitors steal our livelihoods and our fellow citizens rebuild theirs, we'll drift further to the margins of British business and the culture we once enriched.

Still not convinced? OK, maybe you'll believe *Campaign's* Maisie McCabe who, having read my article, concluded: "We should not forget there is nobility in encouraging people to buy great products at a decent price."[40]

If I was running an agency again, I'd have that in four foot-high letters in Reception. Or, in the new era of the kitchen office, stuck just above the ironing board.

Notes

1 Can't Sell Won't Sell

1 *Cannes Conflicted,* Patrick Collister, 12 July, 2019.

2 "Will other brands follow P&G's lead and cut digital ad spend?", Leonie Roderick, *Marketing Week*, 4 August, 2017; "A hard sell for admen", Shannon Bond, Anna Nicolaou and Scheherazade Daneshkhu, *Financial Times*, 25 August, 2017.

3 "Achieving Profitable Growth in Consumer Products: Practical Digital Transformation", Alix Partners, June, 2019.

4 Seth Godin, *Permission Marketing: Turning Strangers into Friends, and Friends into Customers* (New York, 2007), p. xviii.

5 Bob Hoffmann, *Badmen: How Advertising Went from a Minor Annoyance to a Major Menace,* (San Francisco, 2017), p.12.

6 Bob Hoffmann, *Marketers are from Mars, Consumers are from New Jersey,* (San Francisco, 2015), p. 65.

7 "Marketing and Effectiveness News and Releases", The Fournaise Marketing Group, 9 June, 2016.

8 ibid.

9 ibid.

10 Orlando Wood, *Lemon: How the Advertising Brain Turned Sour,* (London, 2019), front cover.

11 "The Crisis in Creative Effectiveness", Peter Field, The Institute of Practitioners in Advertising, 2019, p.18.

12 ibid, p. 25.

13 Wood, *Lemon: How the Advertising Brain Turned Sour.*

14 ibid, p.7.

15 ibid, front cover.

16 "Proving effectiveness of creativity is key to profitable marketing", Russell Parsons, *Marketing Week*, June, 2019.

17 "Marketing and Effectiveness News and Releases", The Fournaise Marketing Group, 21 September, 2015.

18 "Goodbye to likes: What should the new engagement metric be?", Danielle Smith, *The Drum*, 9 October, 2019.

19 "A CEO bringing effectiveness to the marketing sector", *CEO Monthly*, 6 December, 2018.

20 "Mark Ritson: Marketers' only shot at influence is to embrace the CMO title", *Marketing Week*, 25 July, 2019.

21 Why CMOs are only lasting as long as Spinal Tap drummers, Samuel Scott, *The Drum*, 17 September, 2019.

22 "P&G's Marc Pritchard calls for an end to the 'archaic Mad Men model'", Sarah Vizard, *Marketing Week*, 1 March, 2018.

23 ibid.

24 "In-house agencies are here to stay (but they need our help)", Libby Brockhoff, *The Drum*, 2 April, 2018.

25 "CMWoe: why the CMO exodus is a warning shot to agencies", Marc Nohr, *IPA Blog*, 2 October, 2019.

26 "Have we lost the ability to make what we make interesting?" Lucian Trestler, *BBH Labs: R&D Zags for the Creative Industry*, 18 December, 2017.

27 ibid.

28 ibid.

2 Why we've lost interest in selling

1 "Mark Ritson: Heineken should remember marketing is about profit, not purpose", *Marketing Week*, 10 May, 2017.

2 ibid.

3 "Milton Friedman was wrong: movements towards social business are proof", Scott Goodson, *The Drum*, 10 September, 2019.

4 "Milton Friedman and the social responsibility of business", Joel Makower, *Greenbiz*, 24 November, 2006; "The origin of 'the world's dumbest idea': Milton Friedman", Steve Denning, *Forbes*, 26 June, 2013.

5 "Milton Friedman was wrong: movements towards social business are proof", Scott Goodson.

6 "Can Liberal-leaning ad agencies effectively sell to conservative consumers?" Will Burns, *Forbes*, 22 November, 2016.

7 "What it's like to be an ad agency Republican in the Trump era", Shareen Pathak, *Digiday*, 22 March, 2017.

8 "Can Liberal-leaning ad agencies effectively sell to conservative consumers?", Will Burns.

9 Patrick Collister – Anti-Trump Ads at Cannes.

10 Derek Robson, email exchange, 26 October, 2019.

11 "The Empathy Delusion", Andrew Tenzer and Ian Murray, Reach Solutions and house51, July, 2019.

12 ibid, p.13.

13 "Salary Survey 2019: Digital, Creative and Tech", Major Players in conjunction with *The Drum* magazine.

14 "The UK towns and cities with the highest and lowest wages", BBC News, 2 May, 2018.

15 Benedict Pringle, email exchange, 22 November, 2019.

16 Survey conducted: 9 October, 2019.

17 The Copy Club, www.eventbrite.co.uk

18 Survey conducted: 9 October, 2019.

19 Survey conducted: 26–28 November, 2019.

20 "Can liberal-leaning ad agencies effectively sell to conservative consumers?", Will Burns.

21 "Trump's win has ad agencies rethink how they collect data, recruit staff", Alexandra Bruxelles and Suzanne Vranica, *The Wall Street Journal*, 21 November, 2016.

22 ibid.

23 "14 Heartland stereotypes that are stifling brands", Paul Jankowski, *AdAge*, 12 December, 2016.

24 "How brands can navigate today's super-political environment", Patricio Robles, *Econsultancy,* 25 May, 2017.

25 "Trump's win has ad agencies rethink how they collect data, recruit staff", Alexandra Bruxelles and Suzanne Vranica.

3 Why our left-wing bias makes us so intolerant

1 "The Empathy Delusion", Andrew Tenzer and Ian Murray, Reach Solutions and house51, July, 2019, p. 8.

2 Jonathan Haidt, *The Righteous Mind: Why Good People are Divided by Politics and Religion,* (London, 2012), pp. 150–179; "The Moral Mind: Researcher blazes the way in our understanding of moral sensibilities", Harrison Tasoff, *The Current,* University of Santa Barbara, 20 August, 2019.

3 Jonathan Haidt, *The Righteous Mind: Why Good People are Divided by Politics and Religion,* pp. 183–189.

4 ibid, p. 185.

5 "14 Heartland stereotypes that are stifling brands", Paul Jankowski, *AdAge,* 12 December, 2016.

6 Jonathan Haidt, *The Righteous Mind: Why Good People are Divided by Politics and Religion,* p. 194.

7 "Why I left my liberal London tribe", David Goodhart, *Financial Times,* 17 March, 2017.

8 The Empathy Delusion", Andrew Tenzer and Ian Murray, p. 15.

9 ibid, p. 18.

10 "Ask Bullmore: How do I stop a Brexiter colleague from being bullied?" Jeremy Bullmore, *Campaign,* 28 October, 2016.

11 "The Empathy Delusion", Andrew Tenzer and Ian Murray, p. 17.

12 "Labour voters more wary about politics of child's spouse", Connor Ibbetson, *YouGov*, 27 August, 2019.

13 ibid.

14 "Does being a Tory mean I'm not 'woke' enough for love", Charlotte Gill, *Daily Telegraph*, 16 August, 2019.

15 "The rise of flat-shares where Tories are not welcome … so why is the rental market hostile to Brexiteers", Charlotte Gill, *Daily Telegraph*, 19 November, 2019.

16 "Why Liberals aren't as tolerant as they think", Matthew Hutson, *Politico Magazine*, 9 May, 2017.

17 "The ideological-conflict hypothesis: Intolerance among both liberals and conservatives", Mark J. Brandt, Christine Reyna, John R. Chambers, Jarret T. Crawford, Geoffrey Wetherell, *Social Science Research Network*, 6 June, 2013.

18 "Why Liberals aren't as tolerant as they think", Matthew Hutson

19 "How empathetic concern fuels political polarisation", Elizabeth N. Simas, Scott Clifford, Justin H. Kirkland, *American Political Science Review*, 31 October, 2019, Vol. 114, Issue 1.

20 "Nigel Farage exclusive: Advertising? I might fancy it myself one day", *Campaign*, 17 July, 2019.

21 "Just do it: The ad industry should embrace its right-wing roots", Paul Burke, *The Spectator*, 3 August, 2019.

22 @timothylindsay, 29 May, 2019.

4 Why we're saving the world

1 Scott Goodson, *Uprising: How to Build a Brand – and Change the World – by Sparking Cultural Movements*, (New York, 2012); David Jones, *Who Cares Wins: Why Good Business is Better Business* (London, 2012); Jim

Stengel, *Grow: How Ideals Power Growth and Profit at the World's Greatest Companies* (London, 2012).

2 "D&AD launches White Pencil Award", Louella-Mae Eleftheriou-Smith, *Campaign*, 13 April, 2011.

3 "Bill Clinton asks adland to fill brains as well as hearts", Arif Durrani, *Campaign*, 22 June, 2012.

4 https://www.collaborativechange.org.uk> dad-white-pencil-symposium

5 https://www.dandad.org > dad-white-pencil-explained

6 "How purpose took over the 2019 Cannes Lion Festival", Carol Cone, *Fast Company*, 27 June, 2019.

7 "Three big Cannes Lions takeaways marketers can learn from", Penny Price, *Adweek*, 24 June, 2019.

8 "How purpose took over the 2019 Cannes Lion Festival", Carol Cone.

9 "Channel George Orwell and push back against orthodoxy", Richard Huntingdon, *Campaign*, 23 October, 2017.

10 Long may we 'rain': UK advertising at Cannes ... – YouTube https://www.youtube.com > watch

11 *Campaign* goes to Cannes, 18 June, 2019 – film no longer available.

12 Glass Lion | Awards | Cannes Lions 2020 https://www.canneslions.com > awards > good > glass-the-lion-for-change

13 "Glass Lions awards honour campaigns for change that challenge stereotypes", Kyle O'Brien, *The Drum*, 21 June, 2019.

14 *Cannes Conflicted*, Patrick Collister, 12 July, 2019; Libresse:Viva La Vulva by AMV BBDO, www.the drum.com

15 Glass Lion | Awards | Cannes Lions 2020 https://www.canneslions.com > awards > good > glass-the-lion-for-change.

16 "D&AD winner Libresse embraces female taboos with

Viva la Vulva", *netimperative: digital intelligence for business*, 7 June, 2019.

17 Tom Callaghan, email exchange, 23 September, 2019.

18 *Cannes Conflicted*, Patrick Collister, 12 July, 2019.

19 "Can Cannes save the world?", Laura Jordan Bambach, *The Drum*, 4 July, 2019.

20 "Extinction Rebellion warns ad industry: You didn't think we'd forget about you?" John McCarthy, *The Drum*, 17 May, 2019.

21 "Over 20 agencies abstain from fossil fuel briefs in support of Extinction Rebellion", John McCarthy, *The Drum*, 9 July, 2019, "Heading off extinction", Paul Bainsfair, *Campaign*, 4 July, 2019.

22 "Watch: More than 80 creative and media agencies join Global Climate Strike", Martha Llewellyn and Ben Londesbrough, *Campaign*, 20 September, 2019.

23 "China's latest coal mania is alarming but green technology has already won battle that matters", Ambrose Evans-Pritchard, *Daily Telegraph*, 27 November, 2019.

24 "London ad agency changes name in support of Global Climate Strike", Mark Johnson, *Prolific London*, 20 September, 2019.

25 "Growing pain: the delusion of boundless economic growth", Ian Christie, Ben Gallant, Simon Mair, *Open Democracy*, 26 September, 2019.

26 "Shell-shocked adlanders call for action at climate summit", Daniel Farey-Jones, *Campaign*, 27 June, 2019.

27 "Growing Pain: the delusion of boundless economic growth", Ian Christie, Ben Gallant, Simon Mair.

28 "The degrowth delusion", Leigh Phillips, *Open Democracy*, 30 August, 2019.

5 Why clients are embracing purpose

1 "Unilever CEO Alan Jope: We'll dispose of brands that don't stand for something", Stephen Lepitak, *The Drum*, 19 June, 2019.

2 Jim Stengel, *Grow: How Ideals Power Growth and Profit at the World's Greatest Companies* (New York, 2012), pp.1–2.

3 Richard Shotton, *The Choice Factory: 25 Behavioural Biases That Influence What We Buy* (Petersfield, 2018), 96–101.

4 "To Affinity and Beyond. From Me to We – The Rise of the Purpose-Led Brand." *Accenture Strategy Research Report*, 5 December, 2018.

5 "The power of purpose: How Procter & Gamble is becoming 'a force for good and a force for growth' Pt 2", Afdhel Aziz, Forbes, 16 July, 2019.

6 ibid.

7 "To Affinity and Beyond. From Me to We – the Rise of the Purpose-Led Brand."

8 "The power of purpose: How Procter & Gamble is becoming 'a force for good and a force for growth' Pt 2".

9 "Unilever CEO Alan Jope: We'll dispose of brands that don't stand for something".

10 "Reasons to be Cheerful", Caitlin Moran, *The Times Magazine*, 28 December, 2019.

11 Knorr Sustainability Partnership Fund | About | Unilever global . . .
https://www.unilever.com › suppliers-centre › sustainable-sourcing-suppliers
Unilever Sustainable Living Plan | Persil
https://www.persil.com › Home Sustainability
Our purpose | Sustainability | The story of Lipton
https://www.lipton.com › our-purpose

12 "Nudge, nudge! How the sugar tax will help British diets", Anita Charlesworth, *Financial Times*, 19/20 August, 2016.

13 "What science says about discounts, promotions and free offers", *Campaign Monitor*, 3 October, 2019.

14 Bob Hoffmann, *Marketers are from Mars, Consumers are from New Jersey,* (San Francisco, 2015), p.17.

15 "Richard Shotton on brand purpose: 'Marketers have fallen out of love with marketing'," John McCarthy, *The Drum*, 22 November, 2018.

16 *Cannes Conflicted*, Patrick Collister, 12 July, 2019.

17 "Volkswagen: the scandal explained", Russell Hotton, *BBC News*, 10 December, 2015.

18 "Volkswagen profit roars back two years after 'dieselgate'", news@thelocal.de, 24 February, 2018.

19 ibid.

20 ibid.

21 The Unilever Sustainable Living Plan | Sustainable Living ... https://www.unilever.co.uk › sustainable-living › the-unilever-sustainable-l. ...

6 Who's buying the purpose pitch?

1 Chartered Institute of Marketing (UK): Millennials love CSR https://sustaincase.com › research › CIM

2 "Millennial Monetary Theory, part III", Boaz Shoshan, *Capital & Conflic*t, 1 August, 2019.

3 "Labour vote set to hold up among HE staff, THE survey suggests", Simon Baker, *Times Higher Education*, 4 December, 2019.

4 "Millennials are first generation to be less well off as wages decline", Charles Hymas, *Daily Telegraph*, 18 October, 2019.

5 *Academic Freedom in the UK*, Thomas Simpson and Eric Kaufman, (London 2019).

6 "Heineken drops 'open your world' as it launches new positioning", Molly Fleming, *Marketing Week*, 6 September, 2018.

7 "Mark Ritson: Millennials are out; blah blahs are your next target group", *Marketing Week*, 11 November, 2015.

8 "Mark Ritson: Nike's Londoner ad is great, but is the city-focused strategy right?" *Marketing Week*, 20 February, 2018.

9 ibid.

10 "Nike to stop selling shoes and clothing on amazon", Sarah Young, *Independent*, 14 November, 2019.

11 "Adidas bets on megacities", Joachim Hofer, *Handelsblatt Today*, 15 August, 2017.

12 "Mark Ritson: Facebook's segmentation abilities are depressingly impressive", *Marketing Week*, 9 November, 2017.

13 "Facebook's 2016 election team gave advertisers a blueprint to a divided US", Alex Kantrowitz, *BuzzFeed News*, 30 October, 2017.

14 ibid.

15 "A very subtle snobbery", Elizabeth Currid-Halkett, *Spiked*, 2 February, 2018.

16 Pierre Bourdieu, *Distinction: A Social Critique of the Judgement of Taste*, (Abingdon, Oxon, 1984), p. xxix.

17 Rob Henderson, "Thorstein Veblen's Theory of the Leisure Class – A Status Update", *Quillette*, 16 November, 2019.

18 Elizabeth Currid-Halkett, *The Sum of Small Things: A Theory of the Aspirational Class* (London, 2017), p.18.

19 ibid, p.18

20 David Goodhart, *The Road to Somewhere: The New Tribes Shaping British Politics*, (London, 2017), p. 3.

21 "HSBC slammed for controversial 'anti-Brexit' ad campaign", James Warrington, CITYAM, 8 January, 2019.

22 David Goodhart, *The Road to Somewhere*, p. 5.

23 "Clinton: Half of Trump supporters 'basket of deplorables'", *BBC News,* 10 September, 2016.

24 "Liberal Democratic government would put happiness at the heart of its agenda, says Jo Swinson", Andrew Woodcock, *Independent,* 10 September, 2019.

25 "A very subtle snobbery", Elizabeth Currid-Halkett.

26 ibid.

27 'The Empathy Delusion", Andrew Tenzer and Ian Murray, Reach Solutions and house51, July, 2019, p. 7; p. 23.

28 "Why does the Left sneer at the traditional working class?", Paul Embery, *UnHerd*, 5 April, 2019.

29 "Have we lost the ability to make what we make interesting?", Lucian Trestler, *BBH Labs: R&D Zags for the Creative Industry*, 18 December, 2017.

30 "Does the ad industry lack empathy?" Simon Gwynn, *Campaign*, 17 July, 2019.

31 Orlando Wood, *Lemon: How the Advertising Brain Turned Sour,* (London, 2019), p. 30; p. 53.

32 The Empathy Delusion", Andrew Tenzer and Ian Murray, p. 19.

33 Andrew Tenzer and Ian Murray, "Why We Shouldn't Trust Our Gut Instincts", Trinity Mirror Solutions, p. 3.

34 "Car adverts appeal to the young, but older people are in the driving seat", Patrick Hosking, *The Times,* 14 August, 2018.

35 "Salary Survey 2019: Digital, Creative and Tech", Major Players in conjunction with *The Drum* magazine, p.3.

36 *The Aspiration Window*, Andrew Tenzer and Ian Murray, Reach Solutions, June 2020, p. 12.

7 When purpose works – and when it doesn't

1 "How one brave idea drove REI's award winning #OptOutside campaign", Patrick Coffee, *Adweek*, 28 June, 2016.

2 ibid.

3 Thomas Kolster, *Goodvertising: Creative Advertising that Cares* (London, 2012); Joey Reiman, *The Story of Purpose: The Path to Creating a Brighter Brand, a Greater Company, and a Lasting Legacy* (New York, 2013).

4 "BT: It's Good to Talk", IPA Case Study.

5 "It's Good to Talk", Robert Bean, *Campaign*, 10 September, 2010.

6 "Unilever CEO Alan Jope laments the 'woke washing' ads 'polluting' brand purpose", Imogen Watson, *The Drum*, 19 June, 2019.

7 "Mark Ritson: "Heineken should remember marketing is about profit, not purpose", *Marketing Week*, 10 May, 2017.

8 "Heineken drops 'open your world' as it launches new positioning", Molly Fleming, *Marketing Week*, 6 September, 2018.

9 www.starbucks.com, "Social Impact"; www.starbucks.co.uk, "Responsibility".

10 "Starbucks pays £18.3m in tax but £348m in dividends", Rupert Neate, *The Guardian*, 27 June, 2019.

11 Fudge on Tax: Cadbury's US bosses paid just £271,000 in tax despite sales of £1.7billion in UK last year", Simon Read, *The Sun*, 10 October, 2019.

12 "PayPal, Apple, Coca-Cola reject N.C. 'bathroom' law but do business where gay sex and cross-dressing are illegal", Michael W. Chapman, cnsnews.com, 13 April, 2016.

13 www.mrpresident.co; "School Reports 2020: Mr President" *Campaign*, 16 April, 2020.

14 "Cock of Gibraltar", *Nowt Much to Say,* 29 August, 2019.

15 "Is this the end of brand purpose?", Nick Asbury, *Creative Review*, 19 June, 2017.

16 "Libresse *Viva la Vulva*", *Campaign*, 28 November, 2018.

17 "Consumers see 77% of brands as meaningless, report says", Erica Sweeney, *Marketing Drive*, 21 February, 2019.

18 "I don't mind if brands profit from Pride – as long as the LGBT+ community does first", Rosie Hewitson, *The Independent*, 2 June, 2019.

19 "Consumers see 77% of brands as meaningless, report says", Erica Sweeney.

20 "Advertising's untold stories", Bob Hoffmann, *The Ad Contrarian*, 8 December, 2019.

21 "AI: Built to Scale", Ketan Awalegaonkar, *Accenture*, 14 November, 2019.

8 Why we're losing touch with the people who matter most

1 "The good, the bad and the troubling: trust in advertising hits record low", Gideon Spanier, *Campaign*, 30 January, 2019.

2 David Goodhart, *The Road to Somewhere: The New Tribes Shaping British Politics,* (London, 2017), p. xv.

3 ibid, p. 5.

4 Ben Cobley, *The Tribe: The Liberal-Left and the System of Diversity* (Exeter, 2018), p. 63.

5 BBC iPlayer – Wasted on Some, www.bbc.co.uk/iplayer/episodes/p07qf26t

6 *"The Empathy Delusion",* Andrew Tenzer and Ian Murray, Reach Solutions and house51, July, 2019, p.19.

7 David Goodhart, *The Road to Somewhere: The New Tribes Shaping British Politics,* p. xix.

8 Orlando Wood, *Lemon: How the Advertising Brain Turned Sour,* (London, 2019), p. 100.

9 'The Empathy Delusion", Andrew Tenzer and Ian Murray, p. 19.

10 Joan C. Williams, *White Working Class: Overcoming Class Cluelessness in America*, (Boston, 2017), p. 53.

11 *"Hidden Tribes: A Study of America's Polarised Landscape*, Stephen Hawkins, Daniel Yudkin, Miriam Juan-Torres, Tom Dixon (New York, 2018); "Americans strongly dislike PC Culture", Yascha Mounk, *The Atlantic,* 10 October, 2018.

12 "Consumers want brands to heal divisions – now is not the time to sit on the sidelines", Christine Wise, *Campaign*, 28 November, 2019.

13 "Americans strongly dislike PC Culture", Yascha Mounk.

14 "Political correctness battles show we have lost our common purpose", Sophie Gaston, *Daily Telegraph*, 23 August, 2019.

15 "14 Heartland stereotypes that are stifling brands", Paul Jankowski, *AdAge*, 12 December, 2016.

16 Christophe Guillay, *Twilight of the Elites: Prosperity, the Periphery and the Future of France* (Paris, 2016).

17 @timothylindsay, 21 October, 2019.

18 Orlando Wood, *Lemon: How the Advertising Brain Turned Sour*, p. 28; p. 47.

19 "When Trust Falls Down: How Brands Got Here and What They Need To Do About It", Andrew Tenzer and Hanna Chalmers, (Ipsos Connect and Trinity Mirror Solutions), p. 10.

20 www.bbc.co.uk>news>election>2015>results; www.bbc.co.uk>news>election>2019>results

21 "The year of 'woke washing': How tone-deaf activism risks eroding brands", Peter Adam, *Marketing Drive,* 18 July, 2018.

22 Conversation with Jeremy Bullmore, 28 January, 2020.

23 Philip Gould, *The Unfinished Revolution: How New Labour Changed British Politics For Ever* (London, 2011).

24 "What now for the UK's advertising industry?", Brian Carruthers, www.warc.com

25 "A successful ad campaign has revived the fortunes of Marks & Spencer", Mark Sweeney, *The Guardian*, 6 November, 2006.

26 ibid.

27 Patrick Collister, email exchange, 5 December, 2019; "Gay Marriage Victories Give New Life to this Banned Guinness Ad from 1995", Jim Edwards, *Business Insider*, 12 November, 2012.

28 Steve Harrison, *Changing the World is the Only Fit Work for a Grown Man: An Eyewitness Account of the Life and Times of Howard Luck Gossage: 1960s America's Most Innovative, Influential and Irreverent Advertising Genius* (London, 2012).

29 "It's not a principle until it costs you money", Luke Sullivan, *Hey Whipple,* 27 March, 2013.

30 "Has advertising forgotten its brand purpose?", Darren Woolley, *The Drum,* 25 September, 2019.

9 So what would I do if I was you?

1 Claire Beale, "Review of 2019: Adland's existential crisis", *Campaign*, 16 December, 2019.

2 "How purpose took over the 2019 Cannes Lion Festival", Carol Cone, *Fast Company*, 27 June, 2019.

3 Certification | Certified B Corporation, bcorporation.uk/certification.

4 "Watch David Droga's emotional cry to the ad industry at

Cannes Lions", Tim Nudd, *Adweek*, 11 July, 2017.

5   Steve Harrison, *Changing the World is the Only Fit Work for a Grown Man: An Eyewitness Account of the Life and Times of Howard Luck Gossage: 1960s America's Most Innovative, Influential and Irreverent Advertising Genius* (London, 2012), p. 113.

6   "When brand purpose goes wrong", Simon White, *Campaign,* 11 July, 2019.

7   "Dominic Cummings calls for 'weirdos and misfits' for No 10", Rajeev Syal, *The Guardian*, 2 January, 2020.

10 Commercial purpose or social purpose? Adland's response to Covid-19 and the post-pandemic recession

1   "What have we learned in the crisis?", Craig Mawdsley, *Campaign*, 4 May, 2020.

2   "IMF sees great lockdown recession as worst since Depression", Eric Martin, *Bloomberg*, 14 April, 2020.

3   "Almost nine in 10 marketers now delaying campaigns in response to Covid-19", Charlotte Rogers, *Marketing Week*, 6 April, 2020; "Mark Ritson: The best marketers will be upping not cutting their budgets", *Marketing Week*, 6 April, 2020.

4   "Mark Read: 'We must be very cautious about second half of 2020'", Gideon Spanier, *Campaign*, 29 April, 2020.

5   "No UK adland recovery before 2021, adland predicts, Simon Gwynn, *Campaign,* 27 April, 2020.

6   "Survival skills will be key to avoid media's Darwinian cull", Gideon Spanier, *Campaign*, 4 May, 2020.

7   "Build new relationships based on trust and mutual

support", Claire Beale, *Campaign*, 20 April, 2020.

8 "Which skills are going to be most in demand as the ad industry recovers?", Jeremy Lee, *Campaign*, 23 April, 2020.

9 ibid.

10 ibid.

11 "Leadership Lessons: WPP senior advisor and author, David Sable", Stephen Lepitak, *The Drum*, 28 April, 2020.

12 "Ad industry needs to come out fighting for advertising", Gideon Spanier, *Campaign*, 24 April, 2020.

13 DMA – Data & Marketing Association | DMA dma.org.u

14 Advertising Association: Homepage www.adassoc.org.uk

15 D&AD: Global Association for Creative Advertising & Design . . . www.dandad.org

16 *The Copy Book: How some of the best advertising writers in the world write their advertising* (London, 2011), p.367.

17 "How will Covid-19 change the way adland works?", Emmet McGonagle, *Campaign*, 8 April, 2020.

18 "Bank of England 'ready to act' as economy shrinks record 20%", *BBC News*, 12 June, 2020.

19 "Creative Breakthrough: Can marketing truly change the world", Thomas Hobbs, *The Drum*, 17 April, 2020.

20 The Drum's Can-Do Festival Event Tickets | The Dots

21 "CIC UK and the world: How advertising fuels the economy", www.thecreativeindustries.co.uk

22 UKBLM FUND – GoFundMe uk.gofundme.com › ukblm-fund.

23 A Short History of Black Lives Matter – The Real News Network

24 Conversation with Jeremy Bullmore, 28 January, 2020.

25 "Fewer BAME employees and a widening gender pay gap: IPA Census 2020 makes depressing reading", *More*

About Advertising, 29 April, 2020.

26 "Killing the elephant in the diversity room – social class", Lisa Thompson, *IPA Blog*, 14 May, 2020.

27 Telephone conversation with James Hillhouse, 18 June, 2020.

28 "Industry leaders stress importance of sustainability amid 'World War C'", Emmet McGonagle, *Campaign*, 3 June, 2020.

29 "Do brands need to decide which consumers they want to keep?" Simon Gwynn, *Campaign*, June 11, 2020.

30 www.crushfff.com › about

31 Greg Lukianoff and Jonathan Haidt, *The coddling of the American mind: How good intentions and bad ideas are setting up a generation for failure*, (London, 2019).

32 "How will Covid-19 change the way adland works?", Emmet McGonagle.

33 "Adland in lockdown: 'More resilient, adaptive and caring than you ever thought'", *Campaign*, 11 May, 2020.

34 "Build new relationships based on trust and mutual support", Claire Beale.

35 "Brand recovery in a post-pandemic world", Jennifer Small, *Campaign*, 13 May, 2020.

36 "Be More Tory", Andrew Tenzer, *Mediatel News*, 5 March, 2020.

37 "Advertising in recession – long, short or dark: A guide to advertising best practice in recession", Peter Field, *Linked in*, 6 April, 2020.

38 ibid.

39 "Coronavirus and the impact on caring", Office of National Statistics, 9 July, 2020

40 "Unilever: brands must avoid 'opportunistic' behaviour during tragedy", Emmet McGonagle, *Campaign*, 3 June, 2020.

41 "Mark Ritson: If 'Black Lives Matter' to brands, where are your black board members?" *Marketing Week*, 3 June, 2020.

42 "Whose side is Labour on?", Paul Embury, *UnHerd*, 26 May, 2020.

43 "Be more Tory", Andrew Tenzer.

44 Telephone conversation with Craig Mawdsley, 3 June, 2020.

45 "How can advertising be good?", Unpublished article, Craig Mawdsley.

46 Telephone conversation with Stephen Stretton, 18 June, 2020.

47 BT: Tech Top Tips : Work : Saatchi & Saatchi saatchi.co.uk › en-gb › work › bt-tech-top-tips

48 "We wanted to do the opposite of everyone else: How BT is demonstrating its purpose during the pandemic", Sarah Vizard, *Marketing Week*, 22 April, 2020.

49 "Brand recovery in a post-pandemic world", Jennifer Small.

50 "UK ad market slump set to improve slightly in June", Gideon Spanier, *Campaign*, 25 May, 2020.

51 "Advertising in recession – long, short or dark: A guide to advertising best practice in recession", Peter Field.

52 "Mark Ritson: The best marketers will be upping not cutting their budgets".

53 "Lockdown update: How the ad industry can help with economic recovery", Imogen Watson, *The Drum*, 17 April, 2020.

54 "How will Covid-19 change the way adland works?", Emmet McGonagle.

55 www.clearchannel.co.uk › latest

56 www.mailmetromedia.co.uk › news › mail-metro-medi …

57 "Channel 4 offers free use of in-house team 4Creative to entice advertisers", John McCarthy, *The Drum*, 29 April, 2020.

58 "Concerned About Small Businesses Going Bust, Furloughed Agency Staff Start New Shop", Sara Spary, *Adweek*, 23 April, 2020.

59 "Publicis goes fishing", Bob Hoffman, *The Ad Contrarian*, 5 May, 2020.

60 "At the IPA, we tie communication and creativity back to business value", Nigel Vaz, *Campaign*, 15 June, 2020.

61 "Advertising matters. It's time to show people why", *Campaign*, 15 June, 2020.

62 Telephone conversation with Charlie Rudd, 18 June, 2020.

63 *The Aspiration Window*, Andrew Tenzer and Ian Murray, Reach Solutions, June, 2020.

64 ibid, pp.18-19

65 "Ad industry badly misunderstands aspirations of normal people, study finds", Simon Gwynn, *Campaign*, 24 June, 2020.

66 "Even a pandemic couldn't make the public care more about brand purpose", Ian Murray, *The Drum*, 30 June, 2020.

67 "New Commercial Arts' James Murphy: 'We want to be unashamed about what we do'", Claire Beale, *Campaign*, 20 May, 2020.

68 ibid.

69 "Watch: New Commercial Arts co-founders on their mission", Claire Beale and Ben Londesbrough, *Campaign*, 28 May, 2020.

70 "Brand purpose. The biggest lie the ad industry ever told?", Tom Roach, *Blog*, 25 June, 2020.

71 "Coronavirus: Starmer warns of up to three million job losses", *BBC News*, 25 June, 2020

72 One in seven UK workers could be unemployed this year if second Covid wave hits, OECD warns", Ben Chapman, *Independent*, 7 July, 2020.

73 "How can advertising be good?", Craig Mawdsley.

11 Advertising's Somewheres speak out

1 Andy Bunday, LinkedIn comment, 26 September, 2020.
2 Justine Wright, LinkedIn comment, 24 November, 2020.
3 Sarah Mason, email exchange, 4 April 2021.
4 "Who gives a crap, brand purpose and toilet paper with Vanessa Morrish", James Barrow, *The B-Side with James Barrow*.
5 Toby Allen, LinkedIn comment, 4 October, 2020.

12 The clique that's setting adland's agenda

1 "Andy Main is the new global CEO at Ogilvy", *Economic Times, June 23, 2020.*
2 "Episode 27: Tim Lindsay", Ben Kay, *If this is a blog then what's Christmas?,* 12 November, 2020.
3 "Green gold: How sustainability became big business for consumer brands", Judith Evans and Camilla Hodgson, *Financial Times*, 27 November, 2020.
4 "Unilever CEO: 'Woke-washing' is polluting purpose", Gurjit Degun, *PR Week*, 11 June, 2019.
5 Ipsos MORI Veracity Index 2020 | Ipsos MORI
6 "D&AD appoints 'positive provocateur' Naresh Ramchandani as president", Henry Wong, *Design Week*, 9 October, 2020.
7 "D&AD's new president: 'The world is burning and life's not always fair'" Emmett McGonagle, *Campaign*, 8 October, 2020.
8 "Adlanders work long hours because clients don't pay their agencies enough money", Tim Lindsay, *Campaign*, 13 May, 2021.

9   D&AD Awards 2021 FAQs | Global Advertising, Design
    . . . https://www.dandad.org › d-ad-awards-faqs
10 Pentagram partner Naresh Ramchandani announced ...-
    D&AD https://www.dandad.org
11 "Episode 27:Tim Lindsay", Ben Kay *If this is a blog
    then what's Christmas?"*
12 ibid.
13 ibid.
14 Orlando Wood, *Lemon: How the advertising brain
    turned sour*, (London, 2019), p.28; p47.
15 "Puncturing the paradox: Group cohesion and the
    generational myth", Harry Guild, *BBH Labs: R&D Zags
    for the Creative Industry*, 5 August, 2020.
16 New Poll Reveals Free Speech Crisis At Universities |
    CARE
17 "A view from Dave Trott:The politics of humiliation",
    Dave Trott, *Campaign*, October 8, 2020.
18 Rory Sutherland, email exchange, 14 April, 2021.
19 "Almost 40,000 marketing jobs have been lost in UK,
    survey suggests", Gurgit Degun, *Campaign*, 9
    September, 2020.
20 "UK's poor GDP performance rooted in weak
    household spending", *Financial Times*, Chris Giles, 16
    November, 2020.
21 What are the challenges to economic recovery from . . .
    https://houseofcommons.shorthandstories.com ›
    treasur.
22 Economic impact of coronavirus: the challenges of
    recovery . . . https://publications.parliament.uk ›
    cmselect › cmtreasy
23 Households save a record amount of money last month
    | This . . . https://www.thisismoney.co.uk ›
    article-8470423
24 "How the IPA plans to drive agencies' relevance and
    prosperity", Nigel Vaz, *Campaign,* 15 September, 2020.

13 Diversity – has adland missed the point?

1 "Power 100: Brand purpose shines out in the gloom", Gemma Charles, *Campaign*, 13 October, 2020.

2 "The lives of others. To find a way in, we must find the way out of our own", Martin Weigel, *Canalside View*, 8 March, 2021.

3 "Young, diverse and in need of a break; how can the ad industry welcome talent from all walks of life", Shanandore Robinson, *Shots*, 1 October, 2020.

4 Conversation with Anthony Hopper and Simon Goodall, 5 April, 2021.

5 "Brand Jargon", Andrew Tenzer and Ian Murray, Reach Solutions and house51, 2018.

6 Conversation with Dave Dye, 6 November, 2020.

7 Conversation with Anthony Hopper and Simon Goodall.

8 Conversation with Nick Myers, 23 March, 2021.

9 "Diversity: Is the industry doing enough?" Tim Cummings, *Shots*, 12 October, 2020.

10 "UK ad bosses pledge to support black talent in open letter amid George Floyd outrage", Rebecca Stewart, *The Drum*, 3 June, 2020.

11 Nick Myers, email exchange, 21 May, 2021

12 James Hillhouse, email exchange, 24 May, 2021

13 "The ad industry's dirty secret': Why it's time to recast casting", Brittany Kiefer, *Campaign*, September 15, 2020.

14 Population of England and Wales – GOV.UK Ethnicity facts . . .
https://www.ethnicity-facts-figures.service.gov.uk › latest

15 Ethnicity – JSNA Blackpool
https://www.blackpooljsna.org.uk › Blackpool-Profile

16 "England's most deprived areas named as Jaywick and Blackpool", *BBC News*, 26 September 2019; "Blackpool

has lowest disability-free life expectancy in England",
Rebecca Beardmore, *The Gazette*, 24 February, 2020.

17 Britain's diversity is much more complex than it seems
https://www.newstatesman.com › politics › uk › 2020/06

18 Twitter Backlash Against Sainsbury's Christmas Ad –
Influence . . . https://influence.digital ›
twitter-backlash-against-sainsb . . .

19 Channel 4's £1m Diversity in Advertising Award
challenges . . .https://www.channel4.com › press › news
› channel-4s

20 "Mirror on the industry: How diverse and inclusive is TV
advertising in 2019?", Channel 4 Insight and YouGov,
2019.

21 Diamond – Creative Diversity Network
https://creativediversitynetwork.com › 2020/02

22 Deborah Mattinson, *Beyond the Red Wall: Why Labour
Lost, How the Conservatives Won and What Will
Happen Next*, (London, 2020), p.227.

23 "Do people in the UK trust the media?", Conor
Ibbetson, *YouGov*, 16 December, 2019.

14 Fit for Purpose?

1 "Cadbury Dairy Milk and Age UK encourage kind
gestures to solve old age loneliness", Imogen Watson,
The Drum, 9 September, 2019.

2 ibid.

3 Age UK research on impact of the pandemic on our
older . . . https://www.ageuk.org.uk › articles › 2020/10 ›
age-uk . . .

4 "Cadbury celebrates older people by finding fun stories
from their past", Gurjit Degun, *Campaign*, 23
September 2020.

5   £15 million investment boost to chocolate making at
    historic . . .https://b31.org.uk › Areas › Bournville
6   The Drum Social Purpose Awards | The Drum
    https://www.thedrum.com › content › the-drum-social-
    . . .
7   Email from *Campaign*, 21 October, 2020.
8   LinkedIn post, 28 October, 2020.
9   Conversation with Justin Tindall, 23 April, 2021.
10 Rankings | Creative 100 | WARC
    https://www.warc.com › Rankings
11 "Episode 27: Tim Lindsay", Ben Kay, *If this is a blog then
    what's Christmas?,* 12 November, 2020.
12 Paul Feldwick, LinkedIn comment, 8 February, 2021
13 "Meet all the emerging creatives from Cream 2020:
    'Turning hope into action'", Brittany Kiefer, *Campaign*,
    10 September, 2020.
14 "Salary Survey 2021: Digital, Marketing, Creative and
    Tech", Major Players.
15 Amazon reports UK sales rose by 51% in 2020", Rupert
    Neate, *The Guardian*, 3 February, 2021.
16 https://twitter.com/JordanTeicher/status/
    1367662824491728898
17 https://twitter.com/RobinBrown/status/
    1367874052287762433
18 EffWorks – global initiative championing effective
    marketing https://www.effworks.co.uk
19 Talking purpose in business and ethics with Alan Jope,
    Unilever https://www.cliffordchance.com › resources ›
    blogs › jero.
20 "Byron Sharp on why the best response to Covid-19 was
    to stop advertising", Kate Magee, *Campaign,* 24
    September, 2020.
21 "Trends 2021: Selective innovation and getting
    personal", *Marketing Week*, 16 December, 2020.

22 ibid.

23 ibid.

24 "'Traditional marketing practices are over': Danone's CMO on reinventing the function", Molly Fleming, *Marketing Week*, August 7, 2019.

25 Danone's Faber to give up CEO role after investor pressure https://finance.yahoo.com › news › danone-search-ceo- . . .

26 UK Customer Experience Excellence 2020 – assets.kpmg assets.kpmg › 2020/07 › meet-your-new-customer.

27 A 'new normal'? How people spent their time after the March . . . https://www.ons.gov.uk › releases › coronavirusandho . . .

15 Delusion and reality

1   "January's daily UK Covid death toll averages more than 1,000, figures show", Niamh McIntyre, Pamela Duncan, Caelainn Barr, *The Guardian*, 30 January, 2021.

2   Half a million businesses at risk of collapse without more support https://smallbusiness.co.uk › News

3   Nearly 1,000,000 people have lost their jobs since the . . .– Metro https://metro.co.uk › News › UK

4   "Much of what was normal won't return", Nigel Vaz, *Campaign*, December/January, 2020/21.

5   "We shouldn't be looking to get back to agency life as we knew it", James Murphy, *Campaign*, December/January, 2020/21.

6   "Technology doesn't solve problems by itself", Fura Johannesdottir, *Campaign*, December/January, 2020/21; "Creativity is the only way to survive", Sheryl Marjoram, *Campaign*, December/January, 2020/21; "In 2021,

work-from-home-forever realities will set in", Emma, Chui, *Campaign*, December/January, 2020/21.

7 "Samsung Europe CMO on why it's time for marketing to mature", Benjamin Braun, *The Drum*, 16 September, 2020.

8 "Change has to come with empathy. Fierce, uncompromising, empathy", Lucy Jameson, *Campaign*, December/January, 2020/21.

9 "In 2021, work-from-home-forever realities will set in", Emma Chui.

10 "With limitation comes opportunity", Jonathan Emmins, *Campaign*, December/January, 2020/21.

11 @Robertc1970, 3 February, 2021.

12 @Robertc1970, 3 March, 2021.

13 "The lives of others. To find a way in, we must find the way out of our own", Martin Weigel, *Canalside View*, 8 March, 2021.

14 "The revolt of the elites: Have they cancelled their allegiance to America?", Christopher Lasch, *Harpers*, November, 1994.

15 ibid.

16 Deborah Mattinson, *Beyond the Red Wall: Why Labour Lost, How the Conservatives Won and What Will Happen Next*, (London, 2020), p.20.

17 How Race Politics Liberated the Elites – Anti-Empire https://anti-empire.com › how-race-politics-liberated-th...

18 IPA Bellwether: UK marketing budgets continue falling ... https://www.warc.com › newsandopinion › news › ipa-...

19 "Are creative shops on borrowed time?", Kate Magee, *Campaign*, 8 February, 2021.

20 ibid.

21 ibid.

22 "Dentsu's Wendy Clark: 'If I don't use my position to change the face of the industry, shame on me'", Gideon Spanier, *Campaign*, 18 February, 2021.

16 New blood New hope

1 "Crisis triggers wave of ad agency start-ups", Brittaney Kiefer, *Campaign*, 3 November, 2020.
2 "Why planners are breaking free from agency chains", Kate Magee, *Campaign*, 8 March, 2021.
3 "Ex-Mullen Lowe Open duo Ant Hopper and Si Goodall launch consultancy to 'champion the 99%'", Omar Oakes, *Campaign*, 8 October, 2020.
4 Simon Goodall, email exchange, 29 April, 2021.
5 Conversation with Rob Smith, 12 April, 2021.
6 "2020 vision: Why launching an agency mid-pandemic was a good idea", Lee Tan, *Shots*, 18 December, 2020.
7 Conversation with Simon Thurston, 2 April, 2021.
8 "The power of 10: New IPA president Julian Douglas unveils acceleration agenda", Gemma Charles, *Campaign*, 25 March, 2021.
9 Effectiveness Accreditation – IPA https://ipa.co.uk › initiatives › effectiveness-accreditation
10 "The power of 10: New IPA president Julian Douglas unveils acceleration agenda". Gemma Charles.
11 ibid.
12 IPA Effectiveness Awards Winners 2020 – IPA https://ipa.co.uk › awards-events › winners-2020
13 "Diversity in adland: Why Ogilvy is taking a creative approach to new hires", Heidi Scrimgeour, *The Guardian*, 2 February, 2021.
14 State of the Nation 2017: Social Mobility in Great Britain

– Gov.uk https://assets.publishing.service.gov.uk ›
uploads › file

15 "Londoncentric adland: 85% of staff at big six agency
groups are based in capital", Gideon Spanier, *Campaign*,
14 October, 2020.

16 Dave Warfield, email exchange, 29 April, 2021.

17 Kevin Darton, email exchange, 29 March, 2021.

18 Conversation with Michael Hayes, 5 April, 2021.

19 Richard Dudleston, email exchange, 28 April, 2021.

20 Gary McNulty, email exchange, 27 April, 2021.

21 Andy Bunday, email exchange, 24, April, 2021.

22 Chris Woodward, email exchange, 23 April, 2021.

23 Moodvertising – "Burger King France once again steps
up to . . . https://hi-in.facebook.com › posts

24 Potato production in France increased by 3.4% in 2020
https://www.freshplaza.com › article ›
potato-productio..s Potato Harvest Yield & Storage –
Wikifarmer https://wikifarmer.com › Blog › Vegetables

25 "'Women Belong In The Kitchen': Burger King's
International Women's Day Tweet Goes Down In
Flames", Suzanne Rowan Kelleher, *Forbes*, 29 March,
2021.

26 "Yum! Brands CMO on why brand purpose is not
marketing", Manny Pham, *Marketing Week*, 27 April,
2021.

27 Long live the King: Burger King's advertising plays a
different . . . https://www.warc.com › newsandopinion ›

28 "Why advertising should be more Mrs Brown's Boys and
less Fleabag", Kate Magee, *Campaign*, 9 March, 2021.

29 "Adland should stop trying to save the world and start
selling", Steve Harrison, *Campaign*, 10 March, 2021.

30 LinkedIn post, 12 May, 2021.

31 "New Commercial Arts' James Murphy: 'We want to be
unashamed about what we do'", Claire Beale,

Campaign, 20 May, 2020; "We shouldn't be looking to get back to agency life as we knew it", James Murphy, *Campaign*, December/January, 2020/21.

32 "Adlanders work long hours because clients don't pay agencies enough", Tim Lindsay, *Campaign*, 13 May, 2021

33 Sir John Hegarty: The Industry Has Given Up On Persuasion ... https://www.lbbonline.com › news › sir-john-hegarty-th

34 "Red Wall voters to replace 'metropolitan bubbles' on heritage boards, pledges Oliver Dowden", Christopher Hope, *Daily Telegraph*, 15 May, 2021.

35 Suzanne Costello, email exchange, 16 March, 2021.

36 Paul Feldwick, LinkedIn post, 7 February, 2021

37 42courses: Make yourself irreplaceable https://www.42courses.com

38 "Ex-Brewdog staff allege culture of fear at brewer", *BBC News,* 10 June, 2021.

39 "Top 100 Creative Agencies", *Campaign*, April 2021.

40 "We should not forget there is nobility in encouraging people to buy great products at a decent price", Maisie McCabe, *Campaign*, February, 2021.

Index

CPSIA information can be obtained
at www.ICGtesting.com
Printed in the USA
LVHW030724060821
694493LV00007B/744